Fractured Minds

and

Lost Souls

A Collection of Short Stories and Poems

by Anthony Raby

EARTH STAR PUBLICATIONS

Fractured Minds and Lost Souls

Anthony Raby

Earth Star Publications
P.O. Box 267
Eckert, CO 81418

FIRST EDITION
First Printing January 2018

ISBN 978-0-944851-52-4

Printed in the United States of America

Cover painting by Ryan Ulrich
Grand Junction, Colorado

For my mother:
Thanks for that first book.
See what you started?

For my daughter:
Dream big and fearlessly.
Know that I love you.

CONTENTS

.

POETRY

INTRODUCTION

Regret, Self-Forgiveness
and Things

Regret will kill you. You don't know it yet, but it will. Trust me on this, I know. There are people who say they live with no regrets, that they live life to the fullest. I'm not sure that's a real thing.

If you don't know, I have done something terrible in my lifetime. Something I can never undo. Perhaps you know what I did, maybe you don't. No matter. What matters is I did it, I regret it with my whole being, and all that's left is to live until I die. Not a very nice thought, mind you, but it's what I got.

Back to regret killing you, it's a thing. My regret and shame killed who I once was. This death doesn't happen all at once. It happens in bits and starts. You reexamine every choice you ever made, attempting to understand how you arrived here. You perhaps try to blame anyone else, because the pain of placing the blame where it needs to go is too great (it's yourself, by the way). Then this death, as it comes faster and faster, can go in one of two ways: living death or rebirth. Wait, I can hear you say "rebirth isn't death?" No? Say that to the phoenix, to the old soul reborn into childhood, if there is such a thing. Even in a rebirth, there is death of the old man, even if he wasn't that old to start with.

Somewhere along my path, I ended up on the rebirth side. Call it fate, luck, God, what have you. (I prefer God, but some get caught up on that; I don't require others to believe as I do). In this rebirth, something very strange began happening. Parts of the old me were still around. I still looked the same. I have some of the same interests, but there was a focusing, a clarifying. I became more of what or who I should have been. Is that a thing? I don't know. I'm just putting these words to paper, hoping you'll understand what I'm saying.

Either way, I was being reborn. I knew I had to do things. I had to go to school again, so I started that. I knew that the writing I did became a more serious thing, so I did that. I knew I had to love people, and better understand what love really means, so I did that. Along the way, I've been encouraged in all of these things, and my life has been so far the better for it. I can't explain it. I can't take credit for it, but I am grateful to those who helped. That's a thing.

Even after I started growing, I realized there was still something there. A cancerous cell floating in the newborn spirit. After digging around for it, I found it, examined it and found I had a new question.

What is self-forgiveness? Secular people will tell you it's working past your shame and regret and healing yourself, so you can move on. Move on to what? Spiritual people state I need to forgive myself to better accept God's forgiveness or be free from Buddhism's three poisons. I still don't know the actual answer, but I know this: One step to this self-forgiveness is understanding that despite your shame, your wrongdoing, you still have worth. You still have something to add to the world around you. Whether you believe in an all-powerful God or the implacable march of evolution and time, it all starts with the fact you have some value. Now, you may not have value to others, but it is a value to yourself. Do you value yourself? Do you like who you are, or perhaps could be? Do you want to be that person? I think these are the questions that can start leading one on the right path of self-forgiveness.

I'm not there yet, but I'm trying. This book is one of those steps. To say things I want to say, and things I have no idea how to say. To bring myself more fully into the light and to be free. Because that's what writing is: Freedom. Despite being surrounded by cages and bricks, I can be free in this word, in the Word, in any word. So stay awhile, enjoy the stories. Consider what I have to say, or don't. That is also freedom, and above all else, we desire to be free.

"To write is to escape to endless imagination, to play in worlds of your own devising, to be, in a word, free."

— Me

A. Raby
Fort Leavenworth
September 2017

"No man chooses evil because it is evil; he only mistakes it for happiness, the good he seeks."
— Mary Wollstonecraft Shelley

"I am a human being, capable of doing terrible things."
— "Run," AWOLNATION

The Storm

I woke up to the sound of sails flapping in the wind above me. My eyes opened to see those sails set against a muted blue sky. Confused, I looked around, attempting to figure out how I got here. Elise, my new wife, and I were tied down to a battered four-poster bed with old hemp rope. She appeared to be lost to sleep next to me. We were in the middle of an old wooden ship, gently rocking in the waves. Except for the sounds of the ship, it was silent. There was no one in sight.

I vaguely remembered my mother telling me a story about a pirate captain who married. His crew tied him to a longboat with his wife knocked out next to him. The crew flipped the boat in the water to test the captain's love for his bride. His bride was untied and could slip into the water and drown. The captain struggled to free himself and save her. He was barely able to free his arms and hold her as the boat flipped. Once freed, he fought and slew many of his own crew for endangering his love.

I realized this was happening to me. The boat rocked more vigorously. I called out to Elise while I struggled against the ropes, but my voice stayed silent. I could see the churning water on either side of the boat. Elise was sleeping, her face serene, while I was filled with terror. My struggles finally loosened the ropes and freed my arm. I reached out to Elise as the boat flipped into the water.

I sat up with a start, soaked in cold sweat. My heart beat wildly in my chest. I was back in my bedroom with Elise at my side. I took a few deep breaths to calm down and watched her sleep. She lay there, her fair skin glowing in the early morning light. I laid myself next to her and wrapped my arms around her. I kissed her bare shoulder. She stirred and her mouth curled up into a sleepy smile. She turned her head and opened her blue eyes. Their color reminded me of the sky from the dream. I repressed a shudder.

"Good morning, beautiful," I said, causing her to break into a bigger smile.

"What are you waking me up for?" she asked while wiggling her naked body against mine. "Didn't you get enough last night?"

"Just amazed you're here next to me," I said.

I held her tight as we drifted back to sleep.

Sometime later, the smell of bacon and coffee pulled me from my slumber. Elise wasn't in bed, but I could hear her singing with a country song on the radio. I pulled on some sweatpants and a robe and followed the aroma.

"Good morning, love," she chimed as I entered the kitchen.

"You sure know how to wake a man up," I said and reached for the coffee pot.

"There are a few things I know that can work that effect," she said.

She smiled at me over her shoulder. It was a smile I loved, radiant and heart-stopping. I smiled back.

"I know, babe." I grabbed a plate of food. "I'm heading out to the porch. You joining me?"

"Be there in a minute, hon."

14

I maneuvered myself into the bright morning sunshine. I set the plate on the patio table and stood by the railing. I sipped at the coffee and soaked in the sunshine. There couldn't have been a better place at that moment. I heard the door slide open behind me.

"Are you going to sun there like a lizard or eat this breakfast I just slaved over for you?" Elise asked.

"Someone has to enjoy the weather," I said, turning around.

I returned to the table and we fell quiet for a few minutes as we enjoyed the food and each other's company.

"Are we going out on the boat today?" she asked, wiping eggs from her mouth.

"I don't see why not. I'll have to check the weather."

"Already did. It's supposed to be clear all day, according to the forecast."

"Then I suppose we'll have to make a go of it," I said.

Elise gave a little squeak of excitement, stood up with her plate and came around the table. She kissed me, grabbed my plate, and took both plates inside. I watched her go. She somehow knew I was watching and shook her butt as she went inside. I laughed and worked on finishing my coffee. Leaving a cup of joe unfinished is just sacrilege.

Later, we got out of the car and Elise nearly ran onto the docks. I chuckled and followed while lugging a few things from the car. By the time I got onto the boat, she was already below deck. I busied myself with casting off the tie lines and starting up the engine. I navigated the boat out of the marina and hit open water, when Elise came out onto the deck without a shred of clothing. She came over and draped her arms over me while I steered. I loved how much a nudist she could be.

"Thank you, John. Now I can work on my tan," she said.

I slowed the engine and turned towards her.

"And what a beautiful tan it is, along with the rest of you," I said.

We kissed and she laid out on the deck. I cut the engines completely. I grabbed a novel and sat in a chair overlooking the rest of the deck to enjoy the view.

After a few hours, I got up and checked the instruments. The barometer dropped a few degrees and some light cloud cover scattered across the sky. I put down my book and walked over to Elise. I stood there for a moment and watched her. Something about her expression tugged at the back of my mind, but I shrugged it away. I laid down next to her and kissed the back of her neck. The smell of her skin, lightly touched with coconut, woke another part of me. She opened her eyes and turned towards me.

"Oh, hello," she said and pulled me closer.

She must have seen it in my eyes. Time was spent. Love was made. Sleep came again.

I awoke to the dull rumble of thunder, fully aware. I noticed the darker clouds above me. The boat rocked and swayed. Lightning flashed. Thunder cracked loudly, waking Elise with a jump.

"Oh!" she gasped. "Awww, guess it's time to go. Stupid weatherman," she said.

I nodded. She went below while I went to the cockpit. I noted the barometer had dropped even further, and the compass was spinning randomly. Strange. I turned on the GPS, so I could navigate back to the marina. The clouds began to roil, and lightning struck the water. I tried to start the engine. It wouldn't turn over. The GPS could not find a signal, then I turned it off when it told me I was in Chicago.

Elise came back up, dressed and looking concerned.

"The lights aren't working down there. Is the battery dead?" she asked.

"I can't get the engine to start either. I'll go down and check it out. Get on the radio and see if you can reach someone. Good thing the radio has its own battery," I said.

I rushed below. The lightning flashed with enough regularity for me to find the emergency kit with little problem. I could hear Elise trying to raise someone on the radio. I dug out the flashlight and opened the engine compartment. The battery gauge read empty. My heart raced. Elise screamed. I scrambled back to the deck.

"John, look at that!"

Her eyes were wide with fear as she pointed at something behind me. I spun around and saw something wondrous and terrifying. Over the water was something I couldn't explain. Lightning was in constant contact with the water. It was not striking randomly, but two solid bolts were connecting the sea and sky. Between them was … somewhere else. It was not the sea and storm. It looked sunny on the other side.

"John, what is it?" Elise asked, her voice shaky with terror.

"I don't know. Get below and buckle in. The engine is dead and we have no power. We'll have to ride this out."

As she headed down, I turned my attention to the approaching opening. I heard the roar of the water and saw it rushing through the opening. I grabbed the radio handset and keyed it.

"Mayday, mayday. This is John McGrath of the *Calm Refuge*, requesting assistance from the nearest vessel. Does anyone copy?" I asked.

Silence and static. I tried again after a few minutes,

to no avail. The opening was closer now. I went below and buckled in next to Elise. We held onto each other. The crackling electricity got louder, and the smell of burnt ozone was everywhere. All noise grew louder, and as the boat began to tip, I slipped from consciousness. I heard faintly Elise's scream as she slipped from my arms.

Bright light burned my eyes. I bobbed in the water. My eyes adjusted to the light. I was floating on a partially shored piece of the boat. A few yards from me, Elise lay face down in the sand. Movement made my whole body protest. I ached all over, but was determined to check on her. I pushed myself up and crawled through the water. I rolled her onto her side. Her chest moved, but her breaths sounded a little ragged. She seemed alive and okay, if unconscious. My body sagged with relief. I knelt there for a second, then struggled through the pain to my feet and dragged her further onto shore.

Once we were both safely away from the water, I scanned the surroundings. The beach stretched to the horizon on either side of us. Looking behind me, I saw the land soon rose into forested foothills at the base of a looming mountain range. I heard gulls and spotted them circling above a dark spot further down the beach. I already hated this strange coastline. I bent down to wake Elise. She barely stirred and groaned. She was clearly not in much shape to walk, and even though I was not much better, I picked her up and started shuffling through the sand towards the dark spot.

After a few minutes of carrying her limp form, my arms and shoulders burned. I wished I worked out more. The water roared and hushed as each new wave rolled in. The gulls above called out. It sounded like they were complaining

I wasn't dead yet. The air was wet and salty. It hinted at something rotten. I soon saw the dark spot was a shack. I pushed on until I came to it. My body almost collapsed from all the work. I put Elise down. A pain arced through my back.

"Hello?" I called out.

After a few moments, I knocked on the door. I tensed myself for anything. A few minutes passed. No sound came from the shack. Only the endless rise and fall of the sea. I pushed open the door and let my eyes adjust to the darkness within.

A small shack, roughly ten feet by ten feet, it stood just slightly taller than my six-foot frame. It had a hammock strung up on the far side with a small chest underneath it. The shack also had a fireplace on my right and a cabinet and table on the left side underneath a distorted glass window. Next to the window was a spear. No one was inside. I picked up Elise and laid her in the hammock. I was incredibly sore and tired, but I wanted to look around the place first.

I went to the spear and picked it up. It felt heavy, made of some dark, hard wood. It was topped with a sharpened steel tip. It felt reassuring in my hand. I replaced the spear and opened the cabinet. There were jars inside, all filled with water. Some of them contained clams. I tasted the water in one of the jars without clams. It was fresh water. Elise groaned loudly and stirred in the hammock. I turned back towards her.

"Where are we?" she asked.

"I don't know. The coastline doesn't look real familiar."

"Is the boat okay? What is this place?"

"The boat apparently ripped apart when it came through that opening we saw. I was half floating on a piece of it when I came to. You were passed out on the shore.

I carried you up the beach to this shack. Luckily, there's a spear, clams and fresh water here," I said.

"That means someone lives here. They might not be too happy that we've crashed their place. Still, it could be worse. I'm still pretty tired and achy. You?"

"I ache all over and I'm exhausted," I said.

I noticed a thick wooden beam by the door.

"I hope the owner doesn't come back too soon," I said.

I barred the door with the beam on the brackets on the door. Elise found something that looked like a blanket woven of nets. We both stripped out of our wet clothes and laid them out on the table. We made sure the hammock could hold us both, and after a few attempts dumped us on the floor, we figured out how to lay in it. Elise's body heat relaxed me. I fell asleep.

I heard the creaking of wood, the roar of sea swells and the howling of the wind. I became aware of the ship around me, crewmen scurrying to secure lines and bundles of cargo. Still, others were rolling out casks of gunpowder and carrying shot for the cannons. I was helping push a cannon to the railing. The sea around the ship was a violent slate-gray tempest. From above came a cry.

"Movement in the water!"

I looked over the rail and saw a large, dark shape moving just underneath the water. A glistening fur-covered tentacle whipped out of the sea and impaled a man with the quills on its flattened tip. The creature yanked him underwater, his scream cut off.

"Load shot!" someone cried out.

I held a cannonball while another man packed in the powder charge. I rolled the ball inside. The other man was packing the shot down when a tentacle wrapped around him.

I quickly drew my cutlass and hacked at it. It released him and knocked me back from the railing. A mass of tentacles arose from the depths around a shape with rows of sharp fangs. I was on the deck, frozen at the sight of the beast.

"Fire!" yelled the captain.

Explosions rocked the boat as cannon fire blasted out. The foul creature bellowed. Its cry vibrated through water, air, wood and bone. As I regained my feet, it rose higher out of the water. Its silhouette was visible in the forks of lightning above. A tentacle came straight down for me. I heard thunder and saw darkness.

Rumbling thunder again greeted me upon waking. Confused, it took me a moment to regain my bearings. The shack's walls creaked as the wind howled through the cracks. I felt Elise shift next to me. She still slept, but her face contorted in fear and concern. Her arms began to tremble. I watched her expression change to outright horror. I shook her awake as she cried out. She jolted awake in a state of fright and shock, her breath fast and eyes wild. When she realized it was me, she cried and held onto me, her face buried in my chest. We stayed that way for a while.

She stopped crying and faced me. Her beautiful blue eyes were rimmed in red and still wet with tears.

"I dreamt you died. I watched the life drain out of you," she said.

I lay there in silence, unsure of how to respond. Another crash of thunder overpowered the background of the waves.

"Love, I'm right here and I'm not leaving you," I said, holding her tighter against me.

"Good," she said.

I held onto her, trying to quell the uneasiness inside. Were we having the same dream? Why were my own dreams so ominous?

"We should get up and go see how it looks outside. It might not be safe to stay here. At any rate, we need to get some wood for a fire," I said.

"How are we going to start a fire?" she asked as we climbed out of the hammock.

"Rub two sticks together? Maybe there's some matches around here or something," I said.

I unbarred and opened the door. The scene outside was so different, it didn't feel like the same place. The bright sun was replaced with fast-moving dark clouds coming inland from the sea. The waves were much larger and the wind had a sting to it. Lightning danced a deadly ballet across the clouds. I could easily see the waves were going to be a serious problem if they got much bigger.

"That is one nasty-looking storm. Maybe we should head towards the trees on the hills? I don't think it's safe to stay here," Elise said.

"We don't know if there is any shelter in those hills. There could be a whole tribe of cannibals living in there. Besides, it's dangerous to be near trees during a lightning storm," I said.

"You're right. We don't know what's in there, but we do know what's here and what's coming. I'd like to think it's safer among them than here with that storm approaching," she said, gesturing to the incoming storm.

The storm seemed to acknowledge her point with savage lightning strikes on the water. I was frustrated with the choices.

"Fine, but let's gather what we can from this place first. Owner be damned," I said.

I went inside and removed the jars from the cabinet, while Elise looked through the chest. I was removing the last few jars when she whooped. I looked over as she brought a small wooden box to me.

"What is it?" I asked.

"It's called a tinderbox. My grandpa used to use one on our camping trips when I was a little girl." She opened the box. "See? It's full of wood shavings that you use to start the fire. The box keeps them nice and dry. This little black stone is flint. Grandpa would strike this against his knife to make sparks that ignited the tinder."

I took the little black rock and grabbed the spear next to me. I struck the rock to the blade and brilliant sparks erupted.

"Good. This will definitely come in handy," I said.

Elise made a pack out of some nets she found and wrapped the jars in the blanket. She loaded them, the tinderbox, and some clothes she found into a makeshift pack. I grabbed the spear and we headed out. I hated to leave this convenient shelter, but one look at the still approaching storm told me this was the best course of action. The waves were steadily growing larger, reaching the edge of the shack. This storm was likely to wash it away. The storm appeared as an imposing wall of rain, clouds and lightning. The thunder had become a steady, unceasing rumble. We headed further inland.

It took us a little bit of time to reach the trees. With the rapidly failing light and no watch, telling time was impossible. I'm not even sure it would have been the right time anyway. When we reached the trees, the rain fell. Not in some easy sprinkle, but in sheets of water which immediately soaked us again. I muttered a few curses under my breath at the storm.

The wind tore through the trees, bending some severely. I heard branches being ripped from their perches. I looked behind me at Elise. She huddled around the pack, shivering, trying to shield her eyes from the pouring rain. Seeing her shiver in the wind and rain reminded me we needed firewood. I felt a pang of despair as everything around us was already soaked. I picked up what sticks I could, juggling them and the spear.

We came around a hill and found something that both filled me with elation and dread. Set into the side of the hills facing each other were doorways made of stone. The frames reminded me of pictures of Stonehenge. The one on the left was blocked by a large flat stone, while the other was open and dark.

"I think we'll have to hold up in there," I said.

"Fine, but I don't like the creepy feeling I get from them," Elise said.

"We don't have much choice. We need to get out of this rain."

"I know. I still don't have to like it."

I handed her the stack of wood and gripped the spear with both hands. We stepped inside and were enveloped by the darkness. The storm felt muffled in here. We stood there for a few seconds, letting our eyes adjust. It was a small dry area with a large stone platform opposite the doorway. Between the platform and the doorway was a shallow bowl on a stand. To my right, a torch rested in a sconce. I was surprised by how clean it was. It looked as if it had been undisturbed for a long time, yet there was no layer of dust, no debris to show the passage of time.

"I think this is some sort of tomb," Elise said.

"What makes you say that?"

"It just feels that way. I can't place it."

"Well, I don't care either way. It would be creepy, but it's shelter," I said.

Elise put the wood into the bowl. A series of muffled tones rang out as she dumped the wood in. She brought out the tinderbox, and I packed some of the tinder under the pile. I used the flint and spear tip to spark it. With a bit of coaxing and blowing, the tinder ignited and the fire was going. We felt pretty accomplished. The fire popped as the water in the wood boiled. Looking at our meager stack of wood, I realized it wasn't going to last too long.

"I'm going to have to go get more wood," I said.

"I know."

"It's pretty dark out there. You didn't happen to find a lantern or anything like that, did you?"

"No, but there's that torch on the wall," Elise said.

"Oh, yeah."

I pulled it out of the sconce and looked it over. The oily cloth wrapped around the end of it looked usable. I stuck it into the still weak fire to ignite it. After a few seconds, it flared to life, casting light all around.

"This should do. I just hope it doesn't go out in the rain. At least it's died down a little out there. I'll make it back quick," I said.

I grabbed the spear while Elise emptied the makeshift pack.

"Here, you'll need this," she said.

Her eyes had a strange look, but she kissed and embraced me anyway. I headed out the doorway. The storm greeted me, eager to do battle again. Lightning struck a nearby tree. The flash momentarily blinded me. The torch's flame sputtered in the wind and hissed in the rain, but it held on. I tied the pack around me, so I could put wood into it. It looked workable. I walked around the hill and deeper into the trees. I began filling the pack with whatever wood I could find.

Night had come and my flame flickered, throwing the shadows around me in a wild fey dance. Under the larger and older trees, I found some thicker bits of cast-off branches which were still partly dry. After getting enough to fill the pack, I headed back to our shelter. I could see the glow from inside.

Suddenly, a cat's snarl ripped through the wind and rain. I spun around with the spear held in front of me. I couldn't see too far into the woods with the torch in my hand, and I was sure the storm wouldn't have let me see much further anyway. Staying alert, I backed inside, only to have a net hit my back at the door.

"Whoa! It's just me, Elise," I said.

"Did you hear that thing?" she asked, the panic evident in her voice.

"Yeah, it sounded like a big cat. We should be all right in here. Let's get this wood under the bowl, so it can dry out some before we put it in the fire. I need to dry myself out."

We laid the wood out and put a few pieces in the fire. The hissing and popping of the fire was comforting.

"So, John, I really think we're in some kind of tomb. I found a seam in the stone platform. I think it's some sort of coffin," Elise said.

"Um, what?"

We got up and she showed me the line near the top of the platform. I worked the spear tip into it. It separated and a faint smell of rot came from inside. A blue glow came from inside it.

"Do you see that?" I asked.

Elise bent down and peered inside.

"I can't see what it is, but there's definitely something glowing in there," she said.

I wedged the spear deeper and slid the slab aside.

Inside the stone coffin lay a skeleton covered in ancient rusty armor and scraps of cloth. A glowing sword lay on its chest, blade pointed towards its feet. The sword, a few feet long, tapered to a point, with a line of runes etched along the blade. A pile of bones overlapped the hilt of the sword, still trying to grasp it. A thick gold ring set with a large pearl circled one of the bones.

I reached for the sword as Elise grabbed the ring and slid it off the bone. The sword felt surprisingly light. I could feel it vibrating. Elise gasped as she put the ring on her finger.

Her eyes widened with awe at the blade.

"What?" I asked.

"This is crazy. I put this ring on and it tightened around my finger. It fits perfectly. After it did that, I could read those runes as if I've known them all my life," she said.

"Really? What does it say?"

" 'Cry to Berenth and sheath your blade in holy flame.' I don't know what it means, though. I can just read them."

"Berenth?" I said.

The word felt strange in my mouth. I nearly dropped the sword as white fire ignited from the runes and crawled up and down the edges of the blade. Elise and I gaped at each other in wonder.

"Do I dare say the word 'magic'?" I asked.

A low, basso growl cut our wonder short. I whipped around with the sword raised in my hands. Elise grabbed the spear from where it lay across the stone coffin.

The creature filled up the lower half of the doorway. The lightning outside seemed to line its body in miniature bolts. It looked both familiar and completely alien. It resembled a starving puma with black fur and golden eyes reflecting the firelight. It also had six legs and two tentacles growing out of its shoulder blades. The tentacles ended in flattened tips studded with quills. The cat swam around in my vision, making it hard to focus on it. I fought back a wave of nausea and vertigo.

"John, I don't think it's friendly."

"Just stay behind me," I said.

I yelled and jumped at the creature, hoping to scare it away. With a snarl, a tentacle lashed out towards me. The quills tore gashes on my forearm as I threw it up to shield my head. The pain and fear pushed me to charge it. I swung directly at it, but felt the blade ring against the stone floor as if it wasn't there.

"It would really be helpful if you didn't miss when you swing at it," Elise said.

The cat jumped past me into the tomb. Elise and I moved to the other side, shoulder to shoulder. The faint lightning along its skin lit up the tomb.

"How did I miss it? I thought I was aiming right for it. It looked like the blade hit it. It keeps swimming around in my vision, though," I said.

The cat eyed us, looking for an opening to strike.

"I can see it just fine," she said.

The cat flicked a tentacle at us. Elise swatted it aside with the spear. I couldn't tell she hit it, except for the sound. I didn't understand what was going on.

Magic wasn't real.

"Okay, you go after it with that sword. I'll swat the tentacles away from you as much as possible," Elise said.

I nodded and raised the sword in a two-handed grip. I stepped forward as Elise darted in with the spear, already swatting at the constantly moving tentacles. I swung the sword in wide strokes, hoping to catch the creature with some of them. Elise tried to guide me as best as she could, and I felt the blade strike its flesh a few times. I felt the tentacles rake me a few times, but I focused on killing this thing. Each time the white flames seared the creature, it gave an unholy howl. I started feeling a little light-headed.

"I think it's trying to get past you to the doorway," Elise said.

That gave me an idea. I shifted left, to allow it to try to leap out of the tomb. It saw the opening and went for it, while flicking its tentacles at me as it went by. I swung with every bit of strength I could muster. I felt the blade sink into its flank. It landed in the doorway and collapsed. It was breathing heavily and bleeding more from the gash along its side. It soon stopped swimming in my vision and stopped moving. The lightning along its skin faded away.

I was still breathing hard and could only hear the pounding of my heart, though I was partly aware that Elise was saying something. My adrenaline crashed and my legs went out from underneath me. Pain suddenly registered throughout my body. The next thing I realized was Elise holding me. She was still trying to tell me something. I couldn't quite make it out. My feet were cold. She started shaking me.

"John? Come on, John."

I became more aware, yet colder. I looked down to find a long, deep gash in my stomach. A few quills stuck out of the wound. It seemed we both scored a killing blow.

"Nonononononono, this wasn't supposed to happen," Elise said, tears falling, her head shaking.

I took a shallow breath. The cold kept spreading.

"Elise, listen to me. I love you. Nothing will ever change that. I'm sorry I let you down. You're a strong woman; you'll find your way home. Somehow. I'll always love you. This world, our world, or the next."

I felt my body stop. My eyes closed. I felt really warm as Elise's sobs faded.

I awoke again in the middle of the tomb, standing upright. My vision was tinted in shades of blue. Elise had closed the coffin and my body lay on top of it. The daylight outside was extremely bright. I watched as Elise picked up all the items we found and what looked like cooked meat. I noticed the cat's body was no longer in the doorway. I shouted her name. It echoed, but she never responded to it. She walked to the doorway and looked back. She looked weary but determined. She said something I would never hear and walked into the bright sunshine. I tried to follow her. The doorway stopped me as if it was solid stone. Ethereal blue runes lined the door frame.

I stood there for a minute, examining the doorway. The runes along the door appeared to be similar to those on the sword. I pressed my hand against the open air, only to find it as unyielding as the stone around it. I balled my fist and struck it with all the force I could muster. Blue waves of energy rippled out from the impact until they hit the runes. The runes ignited in white light and blasted me back against the far wall. Standing up, I charged the door. Again, I was blasted back. This time, though, it physically hurt.

I went back to the door frame to examine the runes closer. Each time I tried to touch the runes, I felt a strong tingle throughout my being. Frustrated, my rage unleashed in a silent bellow.

I was never leaving. Time lost all meaning.

Note on "The Storm"

This story was started within a few days after my incarceration started. Within the first two weeks, I had most of the story written, then spent five years revising it as I continued learning.

The story is written out of the grief of losing my own marriage. I loved someone very much, then found myself in some very strange, unrecognizable waters, and then lost everything. The end is exactly how I felt sitting in a cell.

The story ends abruptly as it does to share that sense of loss with the reader. The story could readily go on, and I've had test readers ask me where the rest of it was. That's it. I'm sorry if you're one of those readers who wanted more.

The dreams in this story were inspired by some of my own dreams. I'm a very vivid dreamer, and many of my stories and poems have been inspired by, or outright come from, my dreams. Far too often, I've mistaken a dream for reality (even doing the pinch test!) only to wake up, surrounded by these brick walls. A pretty jarring shock and cruel joke, if you ask me.

I almost had this story set on the same beach in *The Drawing of the Three* by Stephen King. I was going to have him succumb to the lobstrosities, rending him to pieces, but I was afraid of any sort of copyright infringement, and changed it. That book is one of my favorites, though, because King manages to make each character speak in such a distinct voice, you almost never need the speaker tags next to the dialogue.

As for the cat thing, I based it off of a displacer beast from *Dungeons & Dragons*. Any *D&D* nerd would likely recognize it, but I felt it made a great incarnation for the storm itself, as I was trying to portray the storm itself as the antagonist.

Fractured Minds and Lost Souls

An Old Friend

The wood beneath you gives a little as you step onto the old bridge. You take a few steps onto it, before you pause at the railing. A duck jumps into the water below, her ducklings quickly following suit. All chatter happily as they cut through the water. Even with the weight in your heart, you can't help but smile at the beautiful little family. You think about the happy moments with your family, but this only makes the weight heavier. Best leave that alone for now. You continue on. Your footsteps echo under the bridge, overpowering the sound of the water under the footsteps. You take one last step.

There, you've left the city behind and entered the wild. Your foot sinks slightly into the soft, springy soil of the island. It smells greener here. Cleaner. Fifteen feet from shore, but the atmosphere's different. You take a deep breath, and put one foot in front of another. You pat the old sign as you pass. It's the pat of an old friend you're glad to see, but never have any time for. No, you're here for an older friend. It's okay, the sign understands.

The ground hardens on the trail as you enter the trees. It's not its fault. You're just another pair of feet it sees nearly every day, but it knows you. It secretly wants to soften for you, to be comfortable for you, but it has those it has to protect. You understand the hardness, the need to protect.

33

The sound of the river muffles, lost somewhere in the trees. They grow close as blood here, standing like an ancient parliament. The trees. They speak in a language you can't hear, casting judgments from long ago. You admire their strength, but you keep moving. You've a got friend to see.

The path meanders on the island. No straight paths. They're not natural. You follow the curves as if tracing those of an old lover. Each bit is familiar, yet exciting and intimate. The sounds of the island blend, fade and rise as you walk. The drones of winged bees and the calls of petulant birds. The splash on an overeager fish and the strange cry of a startled owl. The green is mottled with tree root brown and river stone gray. Patches of color from wildflowers cry out for attention. You admire their brave isolation because they are far from the path. You keep moving. They're selfish anyway.

Now, you're hearing a new sound. A low, unceasing note. Your excitement builds. You're almost there. The note begins to roar as you find the secret, overgrown path. You mutter apologies to the plants as you pass. They need to guard the path, it's best to be polite. This path is even more twisted. Over a gnarled root, around an old trunk beside an older stone. The stone invites you to sit, longing for usefulness. But you don't hear it now over the water's roar.

Then you see it. Your old friend. A lone pebblestone wall. Its original purpose long forgotten. It reaches for the old hydroelectric dam, but it's so far away, never closer. The falling water's roar drowns all else. It is severely displeased about the fall, not so much the flow. You climb on top of the wall. It's solid and wide. It would never let you fall like the water does. You kneel and press your naked hand to its rough surface. I missed you too, it says. You can feel it breathe, vibrating to echo the water's roar. You walk to the end of the wall and sit down. You'll be here awhile.

Here, on this unnatural wall on this natural island, all is perfect. Surrounded by sound, you're cut off from the noise. Five hundred feet from civilization, you're in the middle of nowhere. The weight is gone, just for a time. This is balance.

Note on "An Old Friend"

This whole place is real. It's a little island in the middle of the Rock River flowing through my hometown in Watertown, Wisconsin. It's one of my favorite places in the world.

When I was writing it, I was reading Rothfuss's *The Slow Regard of Silent Things*. In this book, he gives personality and character to objects, even though they never actually move or speak. I loved it. Not to mention, he made up all sorts of wonderful words, some of which I used later, like "emberant." I just wish Rothfuss would come out with book three already!

Fractured Minds and Lost Souls

Opening Time

Amy rested her head on the cool glass of the bus window. It was 3:30 in the morning, and she was headed to a strange place at the request of a friend. The bus was empty, save for the unresponsive driver and a snoring, smelly hobo on the other side of the bus. She was lost in her own thoughts so far, trying to make sense of what she was about to do.

"Next stop, Cherry Street and Eleventh Avenue!" cried the bus driver. The announcement woke up the hobo, who startled awake, wild and wide-eyed. He looked around for a moment, then looked at Amy.

"Whaddya here fer?" he said.

Amy thought about answering, but merely shrugged. It was best not to talk about it.

"Madness it is den," he said.

The bus pulled to a stop. Amy got up and made her way past the hobo. His eyes drilled into her and she was careful not to touch him. She thanked the driver as she got out. The driver just shook his head, closed the door and drove away.

Amy walked in the cool dark of the morning. Cherry Street was still quiet, its windows and doorways lost to shadow. A block from the bus stop, she stood in front of her destination.

The 7/11 was dark, but it was a darkness of two parts.

One was a physical darkness. It was a darkness brought by the absence of people and activity, barely lit by drink coolers. The second part was a waiting darkness, a thing of horror and mystery. This place had become legend through a laundry list of sordid deeds, strange disappearances, and horrific murders. Just recently, three teens disappeared in this area. According to police, the investigation was still ongoing. Lorrie, the mother of one of the missing teens, begged Amy to use her ability to see what happened to her daughter.

Amy was psychic, though she was loathe to use the word. That label always brought to mind the charlatans with tarot cards and crystal balls. She had a post-cognition ability. Sometimes she had to touch objects to see their past. Other times, she just needed to be in the right place. Her trip to Gettysburg last year had been particularly terrifying.

She sighed and leaned against the car parked across from the convenience store. Her breath caught as a vision tore through her mental defenses.

In the claustrophobic darkness, Amy could hear a woman whimpering, her breathing muffled. An unseen mechanism popped and the ceiling jumped. The little light revealed a study in pain and bondage. A young woman, perhaps in her twenties, lay on her side. She was bound, hand and foot, in thin rope, tied with her wrists behind her to her ankles. She was naked, covered in dozens of thin, scabbed cuts.

The ceiling opened, showing a man with no distinct features.

"Ready for round two?" the man said.

His large hands reached in and grabbed the rope between her hands and feet. She tried to cry out, but little more than a muffled gasp came through the gag. She was dragged roughly out of view, then the trunk slammed closed.

Amy snapped back to reality. She found herself crying, shocked at the brutality she witnessed. She backed away from the car, fearful its owner might notice her. She knew she would not enjoy his attention.

She walked around the car to the middle of the street. She wiped her eyes and faced the store. She began to mentally prepare herself now. The last vision caught her unaware, blasting her with the raw emotion of it. She went through the mental exercises she learned to shield her own emotions and ego. The visions would overwhelm her if she wasn't prepared. There were a few times, when she was younger, she spent days, catatonic, after a vision.

Feeling ready, she stepped into the lot and kept her eyes open. She walked in a slow, deliberate stride further into the lot. As she reached the gas pumps, she felt a presence behind her.

It was a dozen feet from her, and it looked like a dark cloud with tentacles roughly assuming a human shape. Occasionally, parts of it would morph into characters she recognized from horror movies that genuinely scared her. Its mouth was impossibly unhinged. Its tongue or tentacle was extended and wrapped a young woman on the ground. It was little Ronnie, Lorrie's daughter, literally being swallowed by this thing. Her eyes were rolled to the whites as the appendage shoved its way down her throat. The swallowing was painfully slow. As the last glimpse of Ronnie disappeared, the thing turned towards Amy. She felt it looking at her. She wrenched herself out of the vision.

She stared at the concrete where Ronnie last lay, stunned. She wondered how she would tell Lorrie what she saw. There was no good way to tell her friend that her daughter was swallowed by a nightmare.

Bright headlights cut through her thoughts as a car pulled into the lot and parked under an "Employees Only" sign. She blinked a few times to clear the spots in her sight. A younger man, dressed in a printed tee and jeans, got out of the car and went to the door. He eyeballed her the whole time. She looked around, trying to decide if she should leave. The clerk unlocked the doors and went inside, turning on the exterior lights. Amy raised her hand to ward off the sudden brightness. The clerk came back to the door.

"Is there something I can help you with? I don't open for another hour yet," he said.

"Could I get some coffee real quick? It's been a full day already," she said.

He eyed her for a moment, his expression suspicious. He relaxed.

"Sure. It'll just take a few minutes to get it brewing."

He held the door open for her. Amy was glad for the company and the chance to check out the store without any customers around.

"I'm gonna look for something to go with the coffee. You mind?" she asked.

"Naw, I don't mind. I got a bunch of things to prep anyway," he said.

He went behind the counter as Amy walked the aisles. Her hands lightly brushed the items on the shelves, occasionally catching unreal glimpses of packagers, buyers and handlers. In the candy section, she smiled at a brief vision of a child begging his mother for the biggest candy bar on the shelf. She paused as she looked through the drinks in the cooler and grabbed a diet soda. As she headed to a small seating area, she grabbed a package of mini-donuts. Before she sat down, she slammed into the past, her mental defenses shattered by a dark and ominous vision.

The vision was inside the store. It was fully dark, save for the light from a circle of candles. A robed figure stood in the center of the open area just outside the circle. The figure held an ancient tome, yellowed with age and decay. Inside the circle, inscribed into the floor, were dozens of arcane symbols. Amy realized she was seeing this from another person's eyes. The view kept bowing to the floor and the chanting echoed in her mind. She saw others doing the same thing. Several figures were around the circle, bowing with arms outstretched. The figure in the center called out in a high, feminine voice.

"We few are met, the candles are set; the blood is collected, pure and unmolested." She raised an ornate chalice and poured its contents into the circle. The arcane symbols collected the thick, dark liquid.

"Old Ones, hear our call. We ask for many to fall. Old Ones, meet our need. We want these to bleed." She threw a handful of scraps of paper into the circle. They fluttered to the floor, flashing names written on them. The papers turned red on the floor.

"Cthulu, Lord of Madness! Vengeance in all fullness, this is what we demand. Sanity lost, we acquiesce." At this, the robed woman called out a string of throat-ripping words. Words no human was ever meant to sound. The candles dimmed as a dark mist formed in the center of the circle. The chanting rose to a fever pitch until all called out.

"Ia Ia Cthulu fhtang!" All extended arms towards the circle, knives in their right hands. Voices rang out once again.

"Ia Ia Cthulu fhtang!" All sliced their left hand, and blood poured freely. Tentacled movement now was seen within the man-sized dark cloud. A cloud that looked too familiar to Amy. Voices demanded one last time.

"IA IA CTHULU FHTANG!"

The cloud exploded in a mass of tentacles. Amy felt them wrap around her. Her throat closed, her body invaded. Pain flared through her being. Consciousness fell away.

Scott drove his car down the empty roads. He had another opening shift. He didn't exactly hate the shift, but at least it kept the old bastard out of his hair. That damned gook must have sprung out of the womb, old and hateful. Kuwabara reminded Scott of the villains from the old Hong Kong chop-sockies he loved to watch. He turned the car onto Cherry Street. Hopefully, the cops would stay away today. They asked a million questions he had no answers to. It was particularly bothersome because the cops were persistent, and it put Kuwabara into an even worse mood.

As Scott pulled into the lot of the 7/11, thoughts of the boss were put on the back burner. Standing in the middle of the lot was a middle-aged woman. She stared blankly at the ground until the headlights hit her.

"What's with all the winos getting here early? Another reason I need a new job," he said to himself.

He turned off the engine and got out of the car. He looked at the woman as he walked towards the doors. If she was a wino, she was pretty good-looking for one. In the darkness, he couldn't make out if she was wearing a ring on her left hand. He saw no new cars nearby, so she must have walked here. Though why she would do that was beyond him, this place was crazy enough. The thought did nothing to ease his suspicions. He unlocked the doors and went to the switches for the external lights. He watched her as he threw them on. She held up her hand to block the light. She definitely had no ring on her finger, and he was between girlfriends. Feeling charitable, he went back to the front door.

"Is there something I can help you with? I don't open for another hour yet," he said, hoping she would come in so he could flirt with her.

"Could I get some coffee real quick? It's been a full day already," she said.

Scott understood. He had those days before and knew what it felt like. Coffee really was the best thing for that kind of day.

"Sure. It'll just be a few minutes to get it brewing." He held the door open for her. Under closer inspection, the woman had an attractive girl-next-door quality and her jeans flattered her ass quite nicely.

"I'm gonna look for something to go with the coffee. You mind?" she asked.

"Naw, I don't mind. I've got a bunch of things to prep anyway," he said.

Scott went behind the counter as she walked up the aisles. He turned on the register and grabbed the keys for the back room. Once inside, he grabbed a variety of breakfast burritos and coffee packs. He went to the prep counter with the armload of things. He turned on the slushie machine and poured the mix into each receptacle. He turned on the roller warmer and stacked all the burritos onto it. He put the coffee packs into the machines and started them. The air began to fill with the aroma of coffee and burritos. He went back behind the counter to finish setting up the register.

As he got to the register, he could hear the woman mumbling. He smiled with understanding, as he also talked to himself on occasion. He always made sure he didn't start arguing with himself. He continued the last few steps of prep for the day's business.

"Ia Ia Cthulu fhtang!" the woman shouted out.

Scott's heart took residence in his throat. He heard her drop something and looked up to see her standing in the break area with her arms extended in front of her. A Coke bottle bounced away from her. He came around the counter.

"Lady?" he asked, deciding cautiousness was a good idea.

"Ia Ia Cthulu fhtang!" she cried out again.

This time, she made a slashing motion with her right hand over her left hand. Blood began pouring from her left hand.

"What the …?!" he said.

He wondered how she cut herself with nothing and moved towards her.

"IA IA CTHULU FHTANG!" she shouted and collapsed.

Scott sprinted the last few steps and caught her before she hit the floor. Her eyes were rolled into the back of her head and her whole body convulsed.

"Oh man, oh man, not again," he said as he laid her down on her side and shoved a nearby peanut package into her mouth, to keep her from swallowing her tongue.

While he was doing this, a man came into the store. Scott glanced at him as the man made his way to the roller warmer. The man was dressed in a green hoodie and had a gnarly biker beard. Scott turned his attention back to the woman. She stopped shaking and relaxed into deep breathing. He knew he had to call 9-1-1. He cursed his luck. This would bring the cops back around. He got up and walked back to the counter, stepping over the green power cord. He paused.

He looked back, realizing there shouldn't be a power

cord in the middle of the walkway. He traced the cord going to the man and up his pant leg. Scott traced it back out the door.

"One thing at a time here," he told himself.

He got behind the counter and pulled out the phone from underneath. He started to dial when the man put two burritos down on the counter. His hands were green.

Scott looked up at the man's face, his confusion melting to unspoken horror. The man wasn't one. It had a face full of writhing tentacles where there should have been a beard. Its eyes were solid black orbs. All of its skin was the dark green of rot and decay. Its voice said something that sounded like a question, except it sounded vowel-less and underwater.

Scott felt something inside him begin to stretch to a breaking point. He blinked.

The thing was gone. He checked the break area, and the woman was gone as well. Nothing was out of place. No blood stained the floor. He looked at the clock. It was just after six o'clock. He made a mental note to see his shrink again, to modify his medications and talk about the hallucinations again. He went back behind the counter. The first real customer of the day arrived not too long after that. The rest of the shift was busy, but uneventful. The cops didn't come in that day, neither did old man Kuwabara.

A week and a half later, Scott woke up screaming. He remembered his missing hour and the two breakfast burritos.

Note on "Opening Time"

This story arose out of a challenge between a friend and me. We had kicked around doing a story together, and he decided he needed practice with the short story form (he is an extremely detail-focused writer). We knew we wanted to do horror, and needed the fiction to take place around an unlikely place for weird stuff to happen. I forget which one of us came up with it, but location became "a 7/11 on Cherry Street."

He wrote the first short story, "Complacency Kills," where three teens are killed by various horror movie monsters, including his beloved Xenomorph (he's a fan of the *Aliens* franchise). Ronnie was originally killed and swallowed by Freddie Krueger.

When I started writing the story, I wanted to explore why these things were happening here, how could these things kill people without it actually being those monsters. I'm a fan of Lovecraftian horror, and decided this would be a good piece to pay direct homage to him. This is also why I kept the dialogue in this story to a minimum.

The "darkness of two parts" is a nod to Patrick Rothfuss, author of the great *Kingkiller Chronicles*. In those books, his prologues and epilogues are written about a silence in three parts, what makes up each individual silence, and how they all rest within one another like some quiet nesting doll, which are creepy.

The story ended up with the dual character split, mostly because I wanted to explore the same scene from two different angles and mindsets. I think it made for a more complete story, and gave me the chance to give the reader more information without breaking from the story to do some exposition.

As for the breakfast burritos, I don't understand why they're in there. They just kind of appeared, and after reading it, I liked it. Who doesn't love those wrapped bits of sausage, egg and cheese? And now I'm hungry.

Moonlight Sonata

He sat down at the piano. The room was quiet and dark. The door to the balcony was open, letting the moonlight shine in. It gave the room a soft, ethereal glow. The moon itself was incomplete, missing a half. He felt the same way. She was gone.

His fingers fell upon the keys, and his right hand began moving of its own volition. Outside, a bell started tolling from the nearby church. The same church where they wed those few short years ago. The same church he last saw her.

As the bells ended, his right hand moving in time with the bells' rhythm, his left hand began moving, pouring out the grief and heartache he felt. The quiet music filled the room, hoping to relieve the void. It almost made him feel like she was right there. The minor keys cut him like jagged shards of a broken wine glass, but he continued playing. She would have liked this piece.

As he played, more intensely now, he thought of all the bittersweet better times. The time when they walked through the garden in the light of the full moon. He thought about their first kiss hidden in the shadow of the new moon. Their love, bright and fierce as an undying sun, now only a dim reflection of light from the farthest stars. Barely visible with no heat.

He missed her. She was his better half, the brighter

half. Now, he was left with the darkness in his being. It threatened to overcome him, but only the music held it back. His fingers moved, the music flowed into the night. A sonata to remember love in a grim-lit night.

All of creation considering, he was glad he had her for even the short time. They loved. She made him better. He could never again be who he was before their time together. She left a little of the moon's light in his life. Loving another woman seemed impossible in this moment, but he knows better. Life will turn the world. It's the way of things. The cycle of the moon.

Note on "Moonlight Sonata"

I wrote this while listening to the classical piece. I wanted to imagine what kind of story would go into creating such a haunting melody. Invariably, it came out with emotions I was pretty familiar with.

Also, this piece made me realize how much influence Poe had on my writing. It shares something with his dark story themes and lost love poetic themes.

Identity/Memory

I stared at the computer, attempting to mentally will it to do the coding on its own. I was startled out of the fantasy by an 8-bit jingle, alerting me to a new email. Caught between boredom and curiosity, I opened my inbox. The subject line read, "Everything you know is a lie."

"What?" I said to myself. "This should be amusing."

I opened the message. In plain text, it read:

Act calm as to not alert anyone, but everyone around you is not who they say they are. You need to quietly get out of there and meet me at the spot where you had your first kiss. You know the place.

— Marc

"Everything you know is a lie," I reread softly.

"Yahtzee!" Dan yelled out in the cubicle over from mine.

I jumped a little, startled by his proclamation. I popped my head up over the cubicle wall.

"What's up, Dan?" I asked.

"Finally got this bothersome line of code to work. I am, of course, a god of the code."

He leaned back in his chair, propped his feet up, and

49

started cleaning gunk out from under his nails.

"Uh, congrats, I guess?" I said. "Can your Holiness debug my crap?"

"Oh no, I'm only god of my own code," Dan said.

"You're a crappy god then."

I felt distracted by the email. My brain kept going back to it. It got me thinking about the oddest things, like why was Dan always cleaning his nails? He was a code monkey. What did he do to gunk up his nails that much?

"You okay, Ned?" Dan asked.

"Huh? Just lost in thought for a sec. Thanks."

I sat back down. I was surprised at how easily the lie came off. I didn't feel well. I was partway to freaking out for some reason. I couldn't understand why this email set me off. It was time to go, if only because sitting here like this was likely to drive me bonkers. I shut down the computer, grabbed my briefcase, and headed down the cubicles.

"Hey-o, Ned? Where ya offta?" asked Carrie, her melodious voice at odds with her massive frame.

I leaned down closer to her, to bring my voice to a conspiratorial whisper. Her cubicle smelled of lilac and light sweat.

"I'm escaping outta here, Carrie. It's pretty nice out. Wanna come with?"

I smiled, playing the part of a man going hooky. Carrie blushed a deep crimson and shook her head. I stood back up fully and projected my voice a little.

"I've got an appointment. Tell Alex for me, will you?"

"Sure thing, Ned. Ya be careful now," she sang back to me.

Her last words sent an itch up my spine as I got onto the elevator. The kind of itch that makes you think someone behind you is about to stab or shoot you. Of course, that might have just been me. Mercifully, the elevator was empty, and I stayed alone all the way to the lobby. Even the lobby was clear, except for the cute redhead guard behind the security desk. I smiled back and thought about asking for her number for the hundredth time. I kept moving.

The sun was bright. I could only see a small part of the sky between the buildings, but not a cloud was in view. I crossed the street to the parking garage.

As I walked through the garage, I could hear squealing tires from somewhere and felt a wave of panic. I nearly broke into a run. What was wrong with me? I hit unlock on my car remote. My gunmetal blue, two-door coupe beeped. I got into the driver side and tossed my briefcase across the front seat. In the rearview mirror, I saw a black sedan drive slowly past. I could barely make out the driver's silhouette, but I could tell he was staring at me. I whipped around to get a better look, but he was already past. I needed to get a grip. I started my car and drove out of the garage.

Out in traffic, it was relatively calm. It was only two in the afternoon. I thought about heading to the park to sit on a bench and just get some fresh air. It would probably do me some good. I usually spent all my time in a cubicle or raiding in my favorite online game.

Before I really understood it, I realized I was driving towards Lee Elementary, to a bench where I had my first kiss with a girl named Ashley. I couldn't remember her last name. Who would? It happened so long ago. Still, the email kept me thinking. Who was Marc? How did he know me, and what was all of this about?

In the midst of this pondering, I noticed the black sedan, but it was a pretty common model. I turned right at the next light and paid attention to see if it continued to follow. When it came around the corner after me, I felt cold all over. I considered the routes between the school and me. The acronym

PACE appeared in my head, and I considered the primary route, the alternative route, a contingency route, as well as an emergency route. I decided on a circuitous route, as I figured it would make sure he was following me.

I started making turns as I drove. My eyes flickered between the rearview mirror and the road ahead. The sedan continued to follow. I sped up, whipped around turns. He still tailed me, almost always three car lengths behind.

Finally, as I neared the school, the sedan pulled off. I breathed a little easier, but couldn't shake the feeling something was very wrong here.

I pulled in front of the school just as it let out for the day. Adults and children were everywhere. Some were getting into cars, other onto buses. Life was just moving on, oblivious to the strangeness developing around me.

I spotted a man with a satchel getting into his car as I was exiting mine. Our eyes met and something passed between us. Recognition, perhaps? I couldn't place it, and the moment passed. He drove off while I made my way through the children. I followed the sidewalk around the school.

I came to the bench, still overlooking the playground as it did all those years ago. I tried to think back how how many years. I couldn't quite remember. I felt a stress headache coming on, so I let it alone. No one was there, so I sat and watched kids chase each other. After a few minutes, a boy with sandy-color hair yelled at me.

"Hey, mister, you dropped something."

I looked down. Sure enough, an envelope with my name on it sat between my legs. It just peeked out from underneath the bench. How had I missed that when I sat down?

"Thanks, kid," I yelled back.

He smiled and raced off. I picked it up and opened it. Inside was a torn scrap of paper with cramped handwriting.

It read:

You were followed here. The black sedan across the playground is from the Agency. I could not stay. You should know they will not let you go easily. If they confront you, trust your instincts. They are better than your memories at any rate. Go to the food court at the Brickyard Mall.

— Marc

I looked up just in time to see the black sedan pull away from the curb across the playground.

"Dammit," I growled.

What in the world was going on? I stood up, shoved the paper into my pocket, and jogged back to my car. I hated this goose chase, but I had to know more at this point. At least I knew for certain that I was being followed. Frustratingly, I earned more questions than answers. Obviously, Marc had these answers. If only I could actually meet him.

I got back in my car and pulled out. My tail soon appeared behind me again. This time, I stayed on the major roads, which were filling up with traffic. It was after three at this point. Traffic slowed things up some, and the sedan still followed. I was beginning to think my car was bugged. I got to the mall around four in the afternoon. It took me ten minutes to find a parking space. There were people everywhere. It seemed Marc was really trying to avoid any confrontation with this Agency. I headed towards the nearest entrance leading to one of the large department stores.

The mall offered a mass of humanity in a tight space. All types of people were within its confines. I watched the people around me as I walked through the store and out into the mall. I walked past a group of teenage girls arguing about which pair of shoes to buy. I walked past a housewife staring longingly at some new toaster. In the mall proper, people milled around, seemingly lost. I felt my anxiety rise as I realized I had no idea what the Agency people actually looked like.

I spotted a mall directory and dodged around a gaggle of moms herding children with various scooters and leashes. According to the directory, the food court was two blocks down and over. I started walking that way.

I was passing an alternative clothing store when I spotted a walking cliché ahead of me. He was tall, built like a linebacker, wearing sunglasses and an earpiece. He was wearing sunglasses inside a mall. Seriously? He was even in a black suit. I turned around, hoping he didn't spot me. Instead, I found another one coming my way from behind me. This guy was dressed the same, but looked much smaller than the other guy. I dodged inside the store.

A teenage girl in black clothing and a spiked collar sat behind the counter and gave me a sullen look as I went back to the clothing shelves. I was pretty sure I was completely out of place in my khakis and button-up shirt. I tried not to care too much and found a spot to watch the entrance while appearing to look at shirts.

Soon, the two suits came into the store. There was the linebacker I first saw, and I could see now the other suit was a short, wiry guy. I ducked down, my heart pounding in my chest. I came here to hide, but I didn't have a real clue as to what I was actually doing here. Thinking through this, I became aware of another part of me. This part was cold and calculating. It didn't seem surprised by any of this. I thought about what Marc wrote in the note.

I heard a squeak on the other side of the shelves. I assumed it was the girl behind the counter. A low voice asked a question. I couldn't quite hear it. I heard her respond in a small voice. Their shoes clicked on the floor as they came closer.

I stood up as they came around the shelves. Scrawny was in front of me and held a taser. Linebacker stood behind me. He might have growled.

"Mr. Sandoval, please come with us," Scrawny said.

It definitely sounded like a command.

"I think I'll decline your polite request," I said.

"We don't want to have to incapacitate you here, Mr. Sandoval."

"Oh, you'd rather taze me in private?" Sometimes, my mouth ran away from me.

I relaxed. I felt the cold settle over me. The mirrored sunglasses Scrawny wore prevented me from seeing his eyes, but it gave me a good line of sight on Linebacker behind me. I glanced down to see Scrawny's finger tightening on the trigger. From here, my body went on auto-pilot.

Just as he pulled the trigger, my hand grabbed a shirt and threw it across the path of the darts. The darts discharged harmlessly into the shirt. Linebacker threw his arms up under mine into some sort of hold. My left foot stomped his as my body twisted. My right hand grabbed his wrist and pulled as my hip twisted, using my hips as a fulcrum to toss him to the ground. My left hand jabbed him in the neck and he went unconscious.

My body reset itself as Scrawny came in with jabs at my head. I noticed he dropped the taser as my hands slapped aside his jabs. My feet brought me closer to him, where my left hand trapped his arm across his body and my right hand drove a fist into his throat. He went down gagging.

The whole thing took mere seconds. I couldn't recall ever moving that fast before.

I stared at my hands and the two men on the floor. I moved around Scrawny, pocketed the taser, and looked at the girl behind the counter. Her expression was a delicate mix of fear and bad-ass awe. I apologized for the mess and left. She nodded.

I made it to the food court without further run-ins. The food court was loud and busy. Mothers, crying children, teenagers gabbing with friends. Some were talking and texting at the same time. I'm pretty sure there are laws against that. I scanned the area and noted a few guys sitting my themselves, looking around.

I had no idea what Marc looked like, and I needed to blend in better. No doubt there were more agents about. I bought a slice of pizza and a soda from a concession counter. I sipped the soda and tried to figure out how to ask any of the guys if they were Marc, without sounding like I was propositioning them. I was saved from possible embarrassment when I passed an empty table with a bulky manila envelope with my name on it. I sat down.

No one seemed to be paying attention to me. I grabbed the envelope and dumped it onto my tray. There was a folded piece of paper, a chip and a wireless earpiece. In the same handwriting as before, the piece of paper read:

Ned, Sorry I could not stay here either. This place is crawling with agents. However, the chip has a video on it that should answer some of your questions. I will try to contact you later.

— Marc

I pulled out my phone and inserted the chip. I put the

earpiece in and made sure it connected to my phone. The chip contained a video file and a document file. I accessed the video file. The man I met eyes with at the school stared back at me. I had just missed him!

"Ned, this is Marc. Before the Agency captured you and scrambled your memories, we were best friends and partners in the Agency. On our last mission in Prague, our handler double-crossed the Agency and pinned it on us. We fought back, then tried to hide when everything went south. They got you while I was able to escape. I am still fighting to clear our names. The attached document on this chip has a list of safe places to hide. Try to stay clear of agents this time. I will find you again. Do not go back to your apartment."

The video showed several photographs of him and me together in various places. Now my fuzzy memory was starting to make sense. I was pissed. I started thinking through what to do next when a scream silenced the food court. I looked up and cursed myself for not paying attention. Several agents were a number of tables away from me with guns drawn. I flung my soda in their direction and dove under another table. I quickly rolled under a few of them, sprang up and ran next to some very distressed, moving bystanders.

"Stop!" a woman yelled.

Blasts erupted behind me. People screamed and dropped to the floor. I dove for cover behind a planter.

My mind was racing. I needed to get out of here. There was far too many people who could get hurt, and these idiots were firing guns now. Ahead of me, there was a service entrance to the halls behind the store. At least I could remove this fracas from public spaces.

I popped my head over the planter. The agents were signaling to each other to surround the planter. I really needed to move. I pulled out the taser, ejected the spent shot, and readied myself to run. I chucked the part in their direction.

"Frag out!" I cried.

I popped up, running for the service entrance. Some of the agents ducked while a few were able to identify what I threw and started shooting at me. Bullets whistled by. I hit the service door at a dead run.

The service halls were dimly lit, claustrophobic spaces. I raced through them, finding them a bit more maze-like than I anticipated. I could hear the agents come crashing through the door far behind me. I came around a blind corner into a bay where delivery trucks dropped off goods for the stores nearby. Luckily, no one was there. I spotted an empty pallet. I picked it up and waited at the corner.

The first agent came around the corner just as I swiveled the pallet around my body into his face. He dropped. His gun skittered forward and I dove for it.

I grabbed it and flipped around while I was sliding across the floor. I started firing at the hallway. The next few agents dove back for cover. I rolled up to a standing position and moved towards the exit door. I fired a few more shots to encourage them to keep their heads down. As I neared the door, it popped open by itself.

I didn't have time to think much about it before I was out the door. I flew across the parking lot towards my car. As I neared my car, something slammed into my shoulder and spun me around as I heard a sharp crack and screams. My feet tripped over each other. As I faded to the darkness, I had time for a final thought.

"Dammit, they had a sniper."

I sat in a chair of some sort. My eyes were still closed, and I could sense something very close around my head.

"Thank you for using the Mental Adventure Recollection Center," a soothing, yet mechanical voice said.

I opened my eyes. I was in a memory implantation booth. On the view screen was displayed "Spy Adventure, Chapter One." I stood up and exited the booth. A cute redhead in a lab coat greeted me with a smile. She looked familiar.

"Did you enjoy your thrilling adventure, Mr. Sandoval?" she asked.

I felt disoriented. I realized I was in a MARC center. I had made an appointment to get away from the office. Being a cubicle drone really was a drain on my life.

"Are you okay, Mr. Sandoval?" she smiled, but it seemed hollow. Everything felt fuzzy again. I sort of remembered coming in and talking to her.

"Uh, yeah, I should be okay."

"Good. I hope you don't mind, but I watched your adventure on the view screen. It was quite exciting. You even had me incorporated into it. I looked pretty good in that guard uniform."

The haziness lifted a bit. I felt a little more sure of myself.

"Yes, you did," I said.

"Would you like to schedule another appointment for Chapter Two?" she asked.

I thought about it for a moment. I wasn't sure I wanted to mess with my memory anymore.

"I'm okay for now. Thank you, though," I said.

"That's fine. I hope you don't mind, but what are you doing for dinner tonight, Ned?" she asked.

She leaned forward with interest, her pale green eyes mesmerizing. I looked her over quickly. Her curves definitely looked inviting, and some small part of me gave a small warning. I ignored it.

"I'm sorry, what was your name again?" I asked.

She held out the name tag on her coat. It only further invited me to look at her chest.

"Jeanine," she said. "I get off at eight. Do you like Italian?"

"Yeah. The little place just down from here?" I asked.

"Of course. Here's my number."

She wrote her number on the back of my receipt. I put it into my wallet.

"I'll see you there at 8:05, then," I said.

"I look forward to it," she said and smiled. It did interesting things to her eyes.

I headed out the door. The bright sunshine glared in my eyes, making me blink. Before I could cross the lot to my car, a black sedan drove in front of me. The driver wore mirrored sunglasses and ignored me as he drove past.

My shoulder began to throb. I had doubts.

Note on "Identity/Memory"

The Corcoran Sun, a now-defunct monthly newsletter published by Freebird Publishers, had a writing prompt and contest. I started writing, and stopped when I got to about 1,200 words. The contest only called for 500 words, so I excerpted the front of it and sent it in.

I won the contest (and a three-month extension on my subscription) for it. It was the first piece I had ever sent into a contest. This story is an expansion and evolution of that original story. This, in effect, made me take my writing more seriously. I started writing a lot more after this.

It was also great practice for writing action scenes. Most things I write don't call for realistic modern action. I usually avoid it because I have a nagging suspicion I'm not describing the movement right.

Also, yes, I admit this is bit of a rip-off of *Total Recall.* I love that movie. The original, mind you—not the remake.

Fractured Minds and Lost Souls

The Letter

Dear Ann,
"Even when all fell apart, I still loved you."
I said this to you in a dream. You smiled in that brilliant and beautiful way I love so much, and then we danced. We spun around the room in a graceful waltz. Soft music filled the whole room. You smiled the whole time and were so lovely. It was easily the best dream I have had in a very long time. When I woke up, I was not depressed as similar dreams have made me. No, I was content, happy even. In the quiet reflection afterward, I heard a still, small voice.

"Now do you understand what I've been trying to tell you?"

I lay there, stunned. As much as the dream was about us, it was also about my relationship with God. It was humbling and awe-inspiring to realize how God is wooing us, broken humans, as much as men woo their wives. This led me to a deeper relationship with Him. This deeper relationship with Him changed my perspective on a few things.

"I want you in my life so much."

For instance, my longing for you has changed. I no longer want you by my side to feel complete. Now, I yearn for us to truly share this adventure called LIFE. It made me better understand what a partner and a help-meet really is.

We are fine by ourselves, but together ... oh. It also made me realize I had unreal expectations of you, how broken I really was. It made me see I was the villain in our story. I released dragons upon our life, and devastation followed them.

I ruined all of it. There was so much pain I caused. It hurt me too.

"This late, is it ever really possible to apologize?"

I write all this to bring my point home. I am sorry for all I did. I hurt you and our children. I know you have your healing process to go through. I know your process is even more of a battle than mine. Still, I wholeheartedly wish for reconciliation, even after all these years. I grasp you have your own decisions to make and God's Will may not lead you back to me. Still, I keep the faith, I pray and I wait. God won't abandon me, I can't abandon Him, and my heart refuses to abandon you.

"I love you. Forever and always."

Your loving ex,
Michael

Note on "The Letter"

This letter is based off of a much longer piece I once meant to write, but could never send. I had this incredible dream, and when I woke up, I was happy from it. Normally, I would wake up from dreams like this feeling awful. It was one of those dreams where I felt like somehow, across time and space, I actually spoke to the other person, felt we communicated. I get this sounds like a bunch of mystic crap, but it's an emotion.

Also, by writing it this way, I left it for the reader to build the outside details of the story. The best short stories make you think after you read them.

Adrift in Noise

It snapped awake to the sound of blaring drums and distorted guitars, head pounding in time with the music. The mouth felt stuffed with weeks-old gym socks. It rolled out of bed to the floor.

"Now the dark begins to rise ..." a voice started singing.

It looked up from a faceplant on the floor and realized it was a person. A person who was eye-level with nearly empty bottles of Coke and Captain Morgan, and that person was me. I patted the bottles.

"Right where I left you."

The voice croaked and wasn't recognizable as speech. I struggled to my feet and took a swig of the flat rum and Coke on the nightstand. I glanced at the clock. 1:24. Judging by the daylight peeking through the coffin black curtains, it seemed to be the afternoon. Breaking Benjamin kept rocking while I stumbled to the bathroom, kicking a pizza box out of the way.

The dinky fluorescent light blinked into existence. I stared at my face in the mirror. Honestly, I looked like I was one good shot of heroin from death, maybe even drowning on dry land.

"It's a good day today!" I said with bare enthusiasm.

The good news was I was leaving today to go see my

sisters. The bad news was there were sixteen hours of driving ahead of me. Ugh.

I stripped and stepped into the shower. After the initial splash of freezing water and subsequent scream, the water quickly heated. Mind fog fully dispersed, it was time to Spock this shit out. Here I am, more than slightly hung over, living in a barracks room away from my wife and daughter. She's probably off visiting family. I'm under investigation by CID. Kicked out of my church. Probably going to prison in the near future. Miss anything?

Nope, that's about right.

I turned off the shower. The iPod had shuffled to quiet classical music. I took a moment to listen to it. The music mixed with the dripping water. No longer held at bay with alcohol, the darkness rushed back on me.

Fucked. I'm fucked. People hate me. I'm watching everything I've worked so hard for, everything I love, turn to ashes. How do people live through this? How do I live through this? It's all my fault ...

I shook my head, trying to shake the chains of thought off, stepped out of the shower, and towel-dried.

"I need some distraction, oh beautiful release," Sarah McLachlan sang.

Nope. Not happening. She wasn't helping. I ran to the iPod and switched the playlist to Linkin Park.

"Forfeit the game before somebody takes you outta the frame and puts your name to shame. Cover up your face, you can't run the race. The pace is too fast, you just won't last."

That's not helping either. I switched over to Hatebreed.

"Now is the time ... for me to rise ... to my feet. Wipe your spit from my face and these tears from my eyes."

Yeah, that'll do. I grabbed a Monster and cold softshell

taco from the fridge and booted my laptop. I loaded Facebook.

More game posts from Mom. An emo-goth post from Sis. Comments and photos from my old *World of Warcraft* guild on last night's raid. Nothing much going on. I finished the taco and shut the laptop down. Time to start getting ready to leave.

Packing didn't take long. I threw everything I figured I would need into a duffel bag, and grabbed my stockpile of Monsters and tacos. It should do for at least ten hours of driving. I headed out the room and past the CQ in the lobby.

"Hey, where you off to?" he asked.

It was a staff sergeant on duty, making sure nothing happened during off-duty hours.

"I'm leaving to drive to my sister's place in Wisconsin. I got some leave, and I'm taking it," I said.

"Did you already sign out from the unit?"

"Yeah."

I produced my leave form, already signed.

"Cool, just do me a favor and sign the CQ book, so I can CYA."

"Not a problem."

I signed the book and headed out the door. I jumped into my truck, plugged my iPod into the stereo, and started it up. "I've Been Everywhere" by Johnny Cash started playing. The drive across post was simple with no hassles. I pulled into the gas station to fill up the tank and go through all the last-minute checks of the engine. Something I've learned about long hauls, always check the engine.

The fill-up only cost a small fortune, and the engine checked out fine. I really needed to do a better job of checking on it more often, but I had been pretty distracted lately. I came out of the gas station a little excited. I was about to drive home for the first time in years. I planned on spending time with my nephew and meeting my newborn niece. I needed time with family, people who loved me. The last few months had been hell, and I needed a break. Halfway to my truck, my phone rang.

"Yeah?" I answered.

"Hey, it's Top. Have you left yet?"

It was my first sergeant. He usually called to check up on me.

"Nope. I'm literally about to, though. Just filled up the truck."

"Well, I hate to tell you this, but the Commander canceled your leave. The lawyers don't want you leaving the area. I'm sorry."

"Uh, okay," I said.

It was all I could choke out. I was shocked. Weeks of planning just dropped down the drain. It felt like the mother of all hammers falling on me. Hell, maybe it was *all* the hammers. It hurt. A lot. I climbed into the truck.

"You there? You gonna be okay? You need anything?" Top asked.

"Yeah, I'll be all right."

I lied.

"Okay. Call me if you need anything," he said.

" 'kay. Thanks, Top," I mumbled.

I hung up the phone and stared out my windshield. I looked at the brick wall in front of me. It looked like shit. Still, I was grateful for it. It didn't care as I sat there weeping. I figured this was it. I'd never see my family again. I'd never get to meet my niece. I couldn't stand the thought of going back to a cold barracks room. Suddenly, the taste of my tears made me realize where to go. Starting up the truck, I cued the iPod to Johnny Cash's "Hurt." As it played, I drove off-post and onto the highway.

Early the next morning, I pulled into a parking lot. I got out my camera and waved to a worker who just arrived to open a store. The color was starting to come to life overhead. I made my way past the storefronts and ignored the deserted boardwalk. Another hour would see it used by people with chew-toy pets and fitness complexes. An hour after that would be the dumb masses, the hawking and the selling. Life. Right now, it suited my mood, but I stepped out to the pier.

The gentle surrah of the waves seemed to take over. I could feel my footsteps through the wooden pier. The infinite horizon continued to grow in color and brightness. In this moment, my camera felt more like a drowning weight than a treasured possession. I pulled it off and set it on the railing. I worried for a moment it could fall into the waves below, but I didn't care. I keenly felt the exhaustion of not sleeping since the morning before and was slightly still hung over from the previous evening.

I needed to just experience this. The darkness told me it was the last sunrise I'd ever see. I pushed it off. It was a weight I couldn't take off, filled with thoughts of regret, shame, prison. They were constant thoughts. It was almost like the background noise of two tweens giggling behind you constantly and you just want to whip around and tell them to shut the fuck up. Unfortunately, I was pretty accustomed to it. I shoved it back for now. It was the best I could do in the moment.

I leaned against the railing and watched the sun come up. My thoughts drifted on the waves to the night before.

Mid-May in Ocean City, Maryland is a weird twilight season. It's no longer the off-season, but vacation time hasn't really kicked up, so there's not a million people. I walked around revisiting places from my vacation just the year before. Before everything seemed to go horribly wrong. Before the accusations. The holidays alone. Feeling the weight and noise overwhelm me, I went into the sports bar next to the hotel.

The sound of the bar was filled with desperation and escape. Basketball games were displayed on two of the TVs, a soccer game was on another. No one cared. This was before the smartphone took over people's minds. Friends and wanna-be lovers filled the booths. Loud and crass. Indifferent to my pain. Fucking sheep.

I sidled up to the bar and grabbed a stool. I ordered something off the menu and a beer. Small favor, they had Guinness. I sipped the beer and tried to pay attention to the game. I didn't give a shit about basketball. I realized it was like golf, people just chasing a ball around. A bunch of overpaid guys chasing a leather ball up and down the court. Soccer, at least, had something like a half-mile long field. Still, every sport was fucking stupid just then. I turned my attention to the rest of the bar.

I realized then I ended up a part of the Bitter Old Fuck Club. The man next to me noticed my attention. A grunt and a nod. It was returned, then I turned back to the TV as the food arrived. I ate, just fuel for the machine. A sponge for all the liquor I was about to drown in. I ordered a Jack and Coke, Coke for coloring. The bartender raised an eye, but said nothing and made the drink. Good bartender. I slammed it. The Jack burned a little, but I liked the pain. I ordered another. I didn't slam it, but I sure as hell wasn't nursing it. I got another. This is when the old guy next to me spoke up.

"Ain'tcha a little young to be drinking like that by

yourself?" he asked.

I considered my answer for a moment. I vacillated between telling him "fuck off" and "nope." I decided on the third "fuck it" option. I let him have it.

"No. I don't think I'm too young. I've done two deployments. Spent nearly eight years of my life in the Army. I'm 26 and losing my marriage, my child, my career and my freedom. I think I'm exactly the right age."

I hadn't noticed how quiet the bar got around me, so my words came out like I was shouting. I turned around and ordered another. This time, the glass was taller and the bartender didn't bother with the Coke. Like I said, good bartender. I got drunk. Someone paid the tab.

I came back to the sunrise in front of me.

"Why am I here?" I asked it.

Funny thing about the Universe. No matter how much Pain you're enduring, it keeps going. It doesn't care, you're just another cog. God can be awfully deaf in those moments. It was then I noticed the gulf between me and God. It was time for an honest conversation between us.

"You know, yeah, I get it. I fucked up. Bad. Big time. Why does it have to cost me everything? Why did you give me everything I wanted, just to let me destroy it all? To hurt everyone I care about? Why haven't you just killed me already?"

He didn't answer me. The conversation was one-sided, so I looked down at the waves then. I thumbed through the iPod to Blue October's "Into the Ocean." I began to ponder thoughts of jumping in then, and letting myself drift and drown.

The thought of drowning myself seemed like an appropriate way to go. A karmic justice of sorts. As much pain as I caused, I would feel all of it as I struggled for air, felt the salt burning my lungs. Legs just kicking away. Eventually drifting off into the blackness. A sort of inner space which reflected outer space. Just gone.

I mentally kicked myself in the balls. I couldn't do it. It was the coward's way out, and I've never been a coward. Besides, what would it all do to her?

I thought about her then. My darling daughter. Every happy moment. I smiled as I thought about last year's vacation. She was into pirates, which was probably my fault, and there was a museum and shop in Ocean City. We spent two hours checking out the exhibits and the gift shop. She giggled as I was goofy; my wife was happily tagging along. To be honest, I think we just enjoyed being around each other and enjoying the things around us. It was one of those rare happy moments which shine for years afterward, just for its simplicity.

I hung my head and cried again. I was alone on the pier. Even the gulls wouldn't come near me. In the growing light, I was surrounded by a palpable darkness which could have killed a random stranger. I looked up and gasped.

The sun broke the horizon, still muted in the brightness by layers of atmosphere. It reflected in the choppy waves, but I didn't see a reflection. It was a perfectly formed flower, made of elemental fire. It was so perfect and ephemeral, I mistook it for a glimpse of God. It could have been God answering me in that moment. It was one of those moments people describe while high. Sober, and not wanting it to go away, I waited. Waited for the world to turn and take it away from me. It did. Life is cruel that way.

Still, the flower had burned into my retinas. The light dissolved the gloom around me, and I felt content, peace for the first time in too many long months. In a dark night of the soul at sunrise, there was still a moment too beautiful to truly capture in words. I had to keep going. Even if it was only to see one of those moments in the future with my daughter. I had to keep going. I already failed so much as a father. There was no reason to continue to fail. I needed to be the father I always should have been. I needed to go back and face the music.

Note on "Adrift in Noise"

I love music. I listen to quite a bit, and my tastes run pretty eclectic. I believe music is important to a stable emotional state. Sometimes you need to just feel an emotion fully, and then move on. Music helps you do that.

This story is pulled from things that actually happened to me. Not necessarily in this order, but it's all true. Perhaps the story is too true, contains too much of my actual story in it, but isn't it always the true stories that have the most impact?

Fractured Minds and Lost Souls

The Hunter

A piercing scream stabs through the air. The Hunter, a young woman with auburn hair styled in a bun, checks her weaponry, and takes off in a dead run towards the sound. The night air is chill and quiet, except for her boots attacking the cobblestone road. The houses are dark and the gaslight lamps' faded golden light clashes with the harsh moonlight. A dog barks as she passes, her breath streams behind her like exhaust from a new locomotive.

She hears people crying in alarm and calling for the Watch. She smiles as she traces the sounds through the winding streets. She turns a final corner and sees lanterns and their people gathering. She slows to a purposeful stride, her weapons of rapier, daggers and wooden stakes all on display. People notice her coming and part, excited whispers mulling through the crowd.

"Did anyone see anything?" she asks, her voice imperious and demanding.

Nearby people, fear apparent on their faces, shake their heads in reply. A slender feminine hand rises above the crowd.

"I found her, Lady Hunter," the hand's voice says.

"Come forward, ma'am. Who did you find?"

The crowd steps back and a thin, haggard woman,

dressed in dirty work clothes and a bandanna, comes closer.

"What did you see?" demands the Hunter.

"I was coming home from my late shift at the laundry, when I decided to visit my friend, Annabelle. She's been having trouble sleeping and fallen on hard times of late, so I knew she would be up entertaining men for coin. When I came to her house here, her upstairs window was open. Her lamp was lit, but I couldn't see any shadows in the light. I called out for her. After a few times, she hadn't answered and I feared for her. Her current work isn't the safest, as we all know. I found her front door unlocked and made my way up to her bedroom. I opened the door to find this Fiend laying over her. I must've surprised him because he tore his face from her neck, and glared at me with the most awful red eyes. There was just blood ... blood everywhere. It was so horrible!"

The laundress begins to sob loudly as one of the nearby women embraces and comforts her.

"Ma'am, I'm sorry you had to discover this state of affairs, but I need you to gather your courage and describe what you saw," the Hunter says, her voice as cold and sharp as the steel on her hip.

The laundress gathers herself back up and takes a deep breath.

"He looked as if he was about the same height as Annabelle herself. He had short brown hair and those horrible red eyes. There was so much blood on his mouth and chin, and he had over-large teeth sticking out from his mouth. I screamed and scarcely saw him move as he fled out the window. He was wearing proper gentlemen's clothes. They were soaked in Annabelle's blood. I don't think he's from around here, Lady Hunter."

The Hunter looked to the nearby house with an open

window and front door.

"Is this the house? Has anyone else been inside?" the Hunter asks the crowd.

An older gentleman in the crowd answers her.

"Lady Hunter, that is the place. Some of us men went inside when we heard the screaming. We helped Ms. Beatrix out of there, but none of us entered the lady's room. T'wouldn't be proper. We had just sent someone for the Night Watch before you arrived."

The Hunter nods and enters the house. She passes all the useless accoutrements of a lived life and heads upstairs. She makes her way to the open door and steps into an abattoir. She must move quickly before the Night Watch shows up.

The air is filled with copper and offal. It awakens a sense of rage and hunger within her. The room is simple and looks like a scene from a penny dreadful novel. The bed and the corpse's clothes are awash in scarlet; the color quickly darkening as the blood congeals. The Hunter walks towards the corpse, careful to avoid the blood pool on the floor. She lifts the eyelids, checking the pupils. Satisfied there is no transformation, she examines the rest of the corpse. Its shift is pushed up above the breasts. The legs are slightly apart, inviting its lover to come to it. The Hunter suppresses a shudder of revulsion and loathing, willing a memory away.

The Hunter steps around the bed to the window. She glances down at the crowd gathered below. She notes another Hunter has arrived and is questioning the crowd, and she steps back from the window. She examines the roof across the lane and sees a roof tile canted and hanging by a nail. Nodding to herself, she leaves the room and finds a window. She opens it, looking at the ground below. The other Hunter's voice grows louder, calling to her from the front door. She opens and ducks through a window, jumping to the ground. She lands lightly and begins to run.

"You! Stop!" she hears behind her. She keeps moving. She becomes lost in her own thoughts, contemplating the fight to come.

Remembering a nearby graveyard, she adjusts her path and keeps her pace. Her quarry has likely taken to the graveyard to hide. The Fiends know enough to lay low after a feeding, thanks to the Night Watch.

Within minutes, the walls of the dead lay before her. The light from the nearby lamps stops at the wall, not daring to cross where it is not welcome. The Hunter runs at the wall, plants one foot on the wall, and vaults over.

She lands, cautious and alert. The silence is oppressive and tangible; thick as blood. She stalks forward, drawing her rapier and a dagger with nary a rasp. The moonlight gives a luxurious silver glow to the headstones and creates deep voids of shadow. She knows her quarry; her predator could lay in one of these dark pools. She picks her walk among the tombstones and comes to the crypts. The shadows deepen here, and she pauses a moment. She glances around, tracing every small sound. Her nostrils flare to sense a smell out of place. She continues moving through the paths between the crypts until she is in front of a particular one. Its light gray stone sharply contrasts with the dark iron door, like a portal of darkness amidst walls of light. The family name sits above the door, a proclamation and a silent witness. She knows this one. She turns the handle and finds the door opens, easy and silent.

"Hello there, little one," says a voice from the past and nightmares.

She spins around, bringing her weapons to a guard position. He lounges on a stone bench alongside one of the other crypts, calm and casual. She sees he is out of easy reach of her silver.

"Fiend, you should be resting inside, not out violating more lives."

"Ah, little one. I can see you are still cross about my gift," he says.

The Hunter laughs, sarcasm woven tightly through her voice.

"Your gift? This curse has made me nearly lose control several times in my too-long life. I've known nothing but discipline and battle since your gift. You stole my innocence and have almost claimed my humanity. For that, there is no acceptance, no forgiveness," she says, the fury and emotion breaking through.

"Who needs forgiveness when you can live forever? Forgiveness is for the dead. If you would just give in, throw away your foolish discipline, none of that would matter. We could be happy," he says.

"There is no happiness for your kind. Only damnation and predation. You hurt those around you. Now that I've found you, let's finish this macabre dance," she says.

"I fail to see where that is helpful to you and me. If I am gone, I can no longer enjoy the tastes of the flesh. You will be out of motivation for your chosen course. You will become a sad husk of yourself," he says, standing from the bench.

"I'll always have plenty of motivation, monster. If I can prevent even one more girl or woman from getting hurt, it will be worth it. There are always more of your kind," she says.

"If that is your decision, then come, little one," he says, holding out his hands, palms skyward.

With a speed that betrays sight, she lunges for him. He backhands the lunge with obvious contempt and steps to the side. She brings the point in low and close to her body, coming around past her stomach, and thrusting again. He sidesteps the strike and hops a few feet away.

"How can you hope to slay me if you cannot hope to hit me?" he says, no sarcasm apparent in his face.

Determination, hard and grim, settles onto her face. She drops the sword and draws another silver dagger. Using the wall behind her, she launches herself directly at him, gleaming tips first. He leaps up and away onto the roof of a crypt, drawing his own steel short blade. She leaps after him and immediately sets upon him in a flurry of slashes and stabs. He dodges and parries the blows, his face full of concentration and concern. She pushes him back further. In a split second lull between her attacks, he sees an opening and drives his blade into her forearm. She gasps from the sudden pain and drops the dagger. He backs off, his face grave. She reverses her grip on the last dagger and cradles her bleeding arm. The blood thirst colors her vision.

"You see, little one? You will never beat me. I have no enjoyment in this. Farewell," he says, turning his back towards her to step off the roof.

She drops her hand to the blade of the dagger. Its touch feels oddly warm. He is about to step off, and stops when he hears her mumble a prayer. She throws the dagger with every bit of her rage, fear, and pain. He reacts too late and it slams into his back, lodging into his spine. He turns as he tumbles off the roof. The Fiend shows his true face as he slams to the ground, a howl of rage and pain fills the night. She walks to the edge and jumps down. She sees him laying there, arms reaching under him, his legs not moving. She pulls a wooden stake from her belt and his howls go sharper still as he knows death approaches. She spots the broken silver blade to the side. His features are sharp, and his eyes are a deep crimson red, nearly black in the low light. His arms flail about as if to ward off the last blow. With a strong, triumphant cry, she drives the sacred wood into his chest. He howls long and loud. His inhuman features melt into all too human features. Features the Hunter knows and hates and loves.

"Caroline?" he asks, confusion and shock draining the color from him.

Her haughty, triumphant expression fades. Her posture drops. A lost and lonely girl replaces the Hunter.

"Oh, Caroline, I'm so sorry," he says, his voice little better than a whisper.

She kneels next to him, all thoughts of anger gone for the moment. Tears run freely down her cheeks.

"I miss you, Daddy," she says.

These simple words tear at his soul as the blood leaves his body. He gathers what little will he has.

"My dear, beloved Caroline. I am so proud of you. You stood as a light against the darkness, even after I hurt you. Do not let what I have done rule your life. Live and love. I pray someday you will ..." He quiets, his eyes darken.

She feels something within her die as he does. She cries with relief, with anger, with remorse, with sadness. She sends her own howl of grief into the sky, her own predator grieving too. She holds him as the cries wrack her body.

As she holds him close, she feels something hard press against her from within his jacket. She reaches into his pocket and pulls out a worn, leather-bound book. She flips open the front cover.

"Caroline, if you are reading this, then you've joined me in this wretched existence or I have passed from it. There is much I need tell you. Apologies, explanations, warnings. I write this in the lucid moments I have free from the monster.

Know that I always loved you ..." It continues on, but she doesn't have the heart to continue reading. She tucks it away and continues to hold his dead body.

Some time goes by. She picks him up, ignoring the violent pain in her arm. She carries him into the family crypt and puts him to rest, closing the door as the sky lightens with dawn's early rays. She walks a little distance and turns back towards the crypt. The birds begin to sing.

"Someday, Daddy. Someday."

Note on "The Hunter"

This story started with a piece of artwork. In a book titled *Vampire Art Now*, there's this piece which features a staked vampire lying on some stone in the rain. The most arresting thing was the little kitten bangle hanging from the end of the stake. I don't remember who painted it, and I think I vaguely remember something in the blurb next to it about a daughter killing her father. It grew from there.

As the story developed, it became something in which I was trying to communicate some understanding about a very difficult subject. I can't go into specifics, for deeply personal reasons. Still, I cried when I first wrote the passage where she stakes the vampire and it's revealed to be her father. While it was a goal for the story from the onset, the emotional buildup to its reveal was a surprise.

I don't often outline my stories, and usually let them develop as I write. I've found the more life I give a character, the more of their own mind they become. I've read others who write about this phenomenon before, and can only agree with them.

Within the story, Caroline shows she doesn't do well with others. At first, it isn't readily apparent why, but then you find she's struggling with her own Fiendish nature that she's not given herself to yet. She also has a hard time with dead people, which is why in the scene with the corpse, it is always referred to as "it," never "her." Even I am not sure entirely why she has this quirk.

At the end of the story, when Caroline says, "Someday, Daddy. Someday," it is supposed to signify she's not forgiven her father for the things he did, but some day she might. As I said, I was trying to communicate understanding.

Fractured Minds and Lost Souls

Hitting the Bottle

A double-bass drum beat coursed through Matt's veins. The crowd was roaring, blood thirsty as always. His intro music played. His trainer, Dave, clapped him on the back, and they stepped out into the spotlight.

The noise in the arena couldn't break his concentration, but he still felt it in the base of his spine. He hopped from side to side as he walked, trying to loosen up and work some of the nervous energy out. The announcer's voice fought the crowd.

"And now for the main card event! Entering the ring in the blue corner, weighing one hundred and eighty-five pounds, standing a mean five feet, ten inches, the underdog in this fight with a record of nine wins, three losses, Matt 'Whiskey' Locker!"

Matt and Dave got into the ring. Matt acknowledged the crowd. A mixture of jeers and cheers went up for him. He paid it all little mind. Dave motioned him to the corner.

"Matt, we've gone over this. Yer tougher than 'im. Ya gotta keep yer defense up 'n ye'll outlast 'im. Jus' be patient. 'E'll get all showboaty if 'e thinks 'e's got ya."

"Thanks, Dave. Have you seen my mother yet?" Matt asked.

"Naw, not yet. But I'm sure she'll be 'ere. She normally

shows up fer yer fights, don' she?"

"Yeah, she does, though sometimes I wish she wouldn't."

Matt's intro music faded out as did the lights. In darkness, distorted guitar riffs and drums started blaring. The spotlight bathed the entrance in light as Matt's opponent came charging into the light. The crowd cheered for him, and the man clearly loved the attention. As he neared the ring, the announcer began again.

"Entering the ring in the red corner, weighing one hundred and eighty-nine pounds, standing six foot even. He's undefeated with ten wins, three by knockout. He's Tim 'Who's Your Daddy?' Freeman!"

Camera lights flashed everywhere. Most of the press showed up to see this up-and-coming fighter. Matt knew he was supposed to be just another guy for Tim to steamroll. Fat chance he'd just let that happen. The referee came into the ring and stepped into the middle. He motioned both men to him.

"All right, fellas. I want a good, clean fight. No low blows. No biting. Come apart when I tell you to. You good?" The referee pointed at Tim.

"Yeah, I'm good," Tim said. His eyes focused only on Matt.

"You good?" The referee pointed at Matt. Matt just nodded.

"Touch gloves and go back to your corners," he said.

Matt reached out his glove. Tim punched it. They moved off to their corners, and as soon as they faced each other again, the bell rang. Tim came quickly out of his corner. Matt put up his gloves and started circling Tim. Tim tested him with some jabs. Matt saw immediately why Tim was winning. The guy was fast. Matt could just track Tim's fist as he moved, but it was startling just how fast he could move. He answered with a few of his own punches, nothing major, just doing his own probes. After a few more circles and jabs, Tim came at him in earnest. Matt blocked the series of jabs, but in focusing on that hand, he missed the incoming right hand. It connected just above his left eye. He felt the skin burst, and he fought to keep his wits about him. He blocked the other punches. Blood began running into his eye.

Matt was already hurting. He blinked away the blood as he tried to return some of the pain Tim already gave him. He got a few shots into Tim's body, but it felt like he was punching a bag full of lead. Matt switched to a more defensive stance. He moved and blocked blows aimed at his head. He threw punches just to keep Tim at some distance. During one of his jabs, he missed Tim's counter. It connected.

The next thing he knew, Matt looked up at his father in the living room. He looked down at his eleven-year-old self. It was the first time he stood up to Darryl, his alcoholic father. His parents had fought all the time. Momma wanted Darryl to be there, for all of them to be a family. Darryl stayed at work or in the bottle. Problem was the bottle always held liquid anger for him. Matt hated watching his parents fight. This time he had enough.

"Why can't you just leave me alone, woman?" Darryl said.

"Because I love you and I want this to stop," Momma said.

"Woman, if you don't leave my ass alone ..." Darryl held up his hand, the threat hanging in the air.

"Leave her the hell alone!" cried Matt.

The words came out of Matt without thought, surprising everyone. His parents looked at him. Momma's eyes reflected worry and love for her only child. Darryl's eyes were glassy, his face just a little expressionless, as if he hadn't quite registered what his son said. Then his features sharpened. Momma saw Darryl's face change.

"Darryl, stop it. Just leave him alone. See? You're upsetting him when we fight like this. He doesn't mean anything by it."

"You shut the fuck up!" Darryl slapped her and she fell, sobbing, to the floor. The sound of the slap echoed in the small living room. Matt's own face hardened in anger, and he raised his own fist.

"Two! Three! Four!" cried the referee.

Matt came back to reality on the mat of the ring, confused. He scrambled to get up.

"Come here," the referee said. He looked into Matt's eyes. Matt stared back.

"You good to keep on?" he asked.

"Yeah, ref. I'm good. I'm fine. Let's go."

"Matt, remember yer trainin'!" Dave said.

"You look all right," the referee said, backing away. "He's good. Fight on!"

Matt refocused on Tim as they met in the middle of the ring. They exchanged blows. Tim landed a jab, but Matt blocked the follow-up punch. It appeared Tim still had plenty of energy to beat on him. Despite Matt's defense, some of Tim's blows still landed, doing damage.

Matt noticed Tim was leaving his left side open. Matt side-stepped another jab and threw his right hand into Tim's body with all he had. He heard Tim's breath rush out of him, then he felt another punch connect with the right side of his head. He went down to the mat again.

Matt was back in time again, looking back up at Darryl, this time from the floor. Darryl stood over him, his right hand clenched in a brutal fist, while his left hand maintained a grip on his bottle. Matt felt blood run out of his nose, but the pain hadn't registered yet.

"What the fuck ya think yer doin', piss ant?" Darryl asked.

Matt jumped back up, staring Darryl down.

"I'm defending my mother, asshole. Don't touch her again."

His mother's gasp seemed loud in the stillness.

Darryl whispered to him, "What did ya say to me, boy?"

Matt swallowed. He knew he was about to get beat. Bad. But he decided right then it was better for him to take the beating than Momma. He glared back at Darryl.

"I said don't fucking touch her again, asshole."

"Ya ain't learned nothin', ya little shit."

Darryl threw another punch and Matt came back to the present, blocking Tim's punch. Matt couldn't remember getting back up. That wasn't a good sign. The bell rang. Matt went to his corner.

"That was a tough round, kid. Ya gotta use yer 'ead to think, not block 'is punches. Ya need to remember yer training. Ya know 'ow to take a punch, give a punch. Do it," Dave said.

Matt's mind wandered as Dave treated the cut above his eye. He remembered catching Momma's eye as Darryl beat him, the helpless look in her eyes. A slap brought him back to the ring, staring at Dave.

"Where the fook ya at? Keep yer head, Matt. 'E's gettin' cocky. Be patient and watch fer 'is overreach."

Matt nodded and stood up. Dave stepped out of the ring and grabbed the stool and bucket.

"Jus' be patient. Ya got this," Dave said.

The bell rang, and both fighters came moving out of their corners. Matt pushed towards Tim, swinging combinations at him. Tim dodged and blocked them.

"What? You can't keep up? You're not fighting some fresh meat, motherfucker. Why're you even in this ring right now?" Tim said.

Matt knew Tim was trying to get in his head, trying to get him to give up.

"Come on! Give me a fight! I could beat you napping. You're not good enough to be fighting me. You're a buster."

Tim came in fast this time, swinging away. Matt backed up from the onslaught, keeping the damage to a minimum. His arms were tired from blocking punches. Tim jabbed a few more times, then sprang back to taunt Matt some more. It was exactly the opening Matt was waiting for. He lunged forward, connecting with Tim's jaw. Tim dropped. The whole arena was silent for that short moment. The referee started counting as the cheers erupted.

"Stay the fuck down, punk," Matt said.

He looked over at Dave, who was nodding his approval. Matt looked at Tim. Blood was pooling out of his mouth, and he still hadn't stirred.

"Nine! Ten! He's out!" the referee shouted.

The flashbulbs began to outshine the spotlights as the photographers took photos of Matt standing over Tim. Dave rushed into the ring.

"Matt, ya did it!"

Matt just smiled. The referee and Dave raised his arms.

"And the winner by knockout in the second round is Matt 'Whiskey' Locker!" the announcer said.

The noise and light of the arena faded to a background as Matt smiled to himself. He thought back to that time, Momma holding him after Darryl left, wiping the blood away.

"I love you, Momma," he had said.

"I know," she said.

Looking back around at the cheering people as he went back to the locker room, he whispered to himself, "Thanks for the training, Dad."

A t the door of the locker room, Dave shook Matt.
"Ya did good. I gotta go talk to some guys real quick. I'll be back. Take yer time, champ."

"Thanks, Dave. Couldn't have done it without you."

Dave walked away as Matt went inside. Matt sat down on the bench next to his locker, the dim light a blessing after the brightness of the ring. He sat there for a second, then he started talking to himself.

"Man, what a fight. Tim was good, if a bit of a dick. I don't know if I would have won that if he hadn't gotten cocky. Still, it feels good winning my first main card fight. I've got to train more. There's definitely going to be more fights from here."

He removed his gloves and started unwrapping his hands.

"Better yet, I didn't see Momma out in that crowd, which means she didn't have to see that beating. Man, that shit hurt. Where was she, though? She's only ever missed a fight for church service.

"Anyway, I haven't thought about that time in a long while. Even though it was the first time I got my ass beat like that, it definitely wasn't the last. I left when I could at 17. Five years later, here I am. I wonder why Momma never left him then, why she endured? I know she's a devout Christian, but God's never answered any of my prayers for her. If He is there, I don't think He cares."

A knock on the locker room door silenced his thoughts.

"Hey, Locker, you in here?" a man said.

"Yeah, come on in," Matt said.

Matt heard the door close and the man's footsteps fell heavy on the floor. Tim stepped into view. Matt sprang to his feet, part of his left hand wrapped and curled into a fist.

"What do you want?" Matt asked.

"Whoa, peace, man. I'm just here to thank you for a good fight. You got outta there before we could speak. I was stupid and you knocked me for it. I just wanted to show you there was no hard feelings," Tim said.

Tim held out his hand. Matt's face and fist relaxed. They shook hands.

"Yeah, no hard feelings. You're a damn good fighter, just don't underestimate the other guy."

"Thanks, man. I appreciate it. You wanna get a drink sometime? Just hang out?"

"We can hang out sometime, but I don't drink," Matt said.

"What?! Every fighter drinks. What are you, some kind of Mormon?"

Matt laughed. "No. My father's an alkie. Bad experiences and whatnot."

"Oh, wait, so why is your nickname 'Whiskey'?" Tim asked.

"My trainer, Dave, started calling me that after he found an unopened bottle of whiskey in my locker. I had to explain to him that it was to remind me to not be like my father."

"All right then. Let's meet up sometime, then."

"Sure, just hit me up on Facebook," Matt said.

"Not a problem. See you around, Matt."

"You too, Tim."

"Thanks for the fight again," Tim said, and then left.

Matt sat back down and finished unwrapping his hand.

He didn't expect Tim to come to him like that. He seemed like an all right guy. With spending so much time on training and working, Matt didn't have much time for friends. He stuck to what he was good at. Friends had been a rare thing for a while.

As Matt sat there quietly, he began thinking about Momma again. The thought brought up an old memory. Momma would read her Bible every day without fail. Darryl wasn't always happy about it, but he left her alone. Matt loved listening to Momma talk about what she was reading. She would just come alive and was so passionate about what she read. He was happy because she was happy. One day, Matt went and bothered Momma during her reading.

"What are you reading today, Mama?" Matt said.

"I'm reading in the Book of Proverbs. It's a book where a king named Solomon shared wisdom with his son. For example, 'My son, if sinners entice thee, consent thou not. If they say, come with me, let us lay wait for blood, let us lurk privily for the innocent without cause: let us swallow them up alive as the grave; and whole, as they that go down into the pit: We shall find all precious substance, we shall fill our houses with spoil: cast in thy lot among us; let us all have one purse: My son, walk not thou in the way with them; Refrain thy foot from their path: for their feet run to evil, and make haste to shed blood,' " Momma read.

"Uh, what does any of that mean?" Matt asked.

Momma laughed.

"It means if someone invites you for bouts of armed robbery, don't join them. It's bad for everyone involved."

"Seems like a long way to put that."

"The Bible's kinda like that, Mattie."

"Well, what else does it say?"

"I'll read some more, you listen. 'My son, if thou wilt

receive my words, and hide my commandants with thee; so that thou incline thine ear unto wisdom …"

Matt couldn't keep the smile from his face as he came out of the memory. He started talking to himself again.

"Momma never got preachy. Even when I started moving away from God, she would tell me about what she was reading. She would get so passionate and wrapped up in it sometimes, I couldn't tell her I didn't want to hear about it. I think I'll call her when I get back to the apartment, find out what she's up to."

Matt changed into some shorts and a hooded sweatshirt. He heard the door burst open suddenly, making him jump.

"Matt, ya in 'ere still?" Dave asked.

"Yeah, I'm back here."

Dave came around the bank of lockers, still clearly excited. "There 'e is! Da champ! Da man! That was a 'elluva fight, Matt.

"Ya did good, kid. Real good. Kept yer head in there. Took all that punishment. Made us a good bit o' money too. Already got more promoters wantin' ta set up fights. This is da start, my boy. Only da start."

"Thanks, Dave."

Dave looked at Matt thoughtfully.

"W'at ya thinkin' about? I can tell w'en yer 'ead's elsewhere."

"Memories. I don't know. Just seems like a bunch of memories are popping up tonight."

"Memories, huh? I remember w'en ya first walked in my gym. An angry kid lookin' to use my punchin' bag for a bit. I sat there and jus' watched ya w'ale on da thing. So much rage, anger. Ya know w'at's da positive side of rage and anger?" Dave asked.

Matt thought about it for a second.

"No. What?"

"Passion. Focus. Ya got 'em. In spades. So I sat there watchin' ya. Figured ya needed a good outlet fer all that. I offered ta train ya. One's da best choices I've done in a good bit."

Dave shook Matt a bit. A knock came on the door.

"Anyone here?" a man's voice came back.

"Yeah, we're back 'ere," Dave said.

Something about the voice sounded familiar, but Matt couldn't quite place it. The footsteps came around, bringing Darryl. He wore a shabby suit, looking haggard. Matt jumped to his feet while Dave inserted himself between the two men.

"What the hell do you want? What the fuck are you doing here?" Matt asked.

"W'oa, Matt. Easy-like now," Dave said.

"I'm sorry, son. I saw your fight. You pulled a good comeback out there," Darryl said.

"I don't fucking care what you think," Matt said.

"I deserve that. Lord knows I deserve that. But please listen just a moment ..."

"No! I don't want to hear anything you have to say. What are you here for? You looking for money to booze?"

"No, son, no. I gave that up. I got saved. Cleaned up."

"Yeah, right. You 'found Jesus,' and now everything's all better? Bullshit. I don't begrudge Momma her religion, but I ain't buying it coming from you."

"Matt, listen. It's about your mother. She collapsed earlier today, and we couldn't get a message to you. By the time I got here, your fight was just about to start, and there was no way I could get to you until now. She's in the hospital. The doctors don't know what's wrong with her yet, and they're saying it may be a coma."

Matt sank back down to the bench. As the tears began to fall, his mind shifted back to an earlier time.

Matt sat at the kitchen table, working on his English homework. He sighed in exasperation at the subject, when Momma walked up.

"What are you working on, hon?" Momma asked.

"I have to write an essay about this book, *Flowers for Algernon*."

"Well, what's it about?"

"It's about Charlie Gordon, who's a retard that undergoes a surgery that makes him three times smarter. It's written like a journal. He befriends a mouse that was another test subject with the same operation. Towards the end, he discovers he's going to regress back to being a retard. I have to write an essay about how I relate to Charlie," Matt said.

"So how do you feel you relate to him?"

"That's just it. I don't know. He seems frustrated a lot, though."

"Really? You can't relate to his frustration? Don't you feel frustrated sometimes?" Momma asked.

"Sure, but it's not the same. He's frustrated because he doesn't know or he can't do something. I get frustrated because I just feel so ... powerless."

Momma sat down at the table across from Matt.

"Hon, that's the same feeling. Not being able to do something is feeling powerless. Frustration is frustration. No matter what it's about. I feel frustrated with your father all the time, but I deal with that by praying to God for him."

"I'm frustrated with Dad, too, but I feel like God's not listening to me, so I'm frustrated with God, too."

"Sounds like you have just as much frustration as Charlie does. Why don't you write about how you relate to

Charlie's frustration because of the frustration you feel every day? Use some examples from the book and compare them with some from your life."

"You know, that's a pretty good idea. Thanks for the help, Momma."

"Of course, Mattie. I'm always here to help," Momma said.

Matt came back from the past.

"But how? I just talked to her earlier today. She sounded fine then. Damn it! How can I believe God cleaned you up when He can't even treat Momma right? All those times I prayed for her when you would hit her, and now He's gonna take her away from me?"

Darryl moved towards Matt.

"I'm sorry, son. I don't even know what to tell you right now," Darryl said.

Matt quickly got up, keeping Darryl at arm's length.

"No, don't touch me. I'll go see her. You've done your job. Thanks for that. I've got nothing else to say to you right now. Dave, can you drive me to the hospital?" Matt asked.

"Sure, Matt. Sure," Dave said.

Matt grabbed his bag and turned away from his father to leave the locker room. Darryl just stood there, looking defeated. Dave gave him a hard look, then followed after Matt. Darryl sat down on the bench. His own tears flowed then, through the hands covering his face.

"Lord, I'm so sorry," he said.

Matt exited the elevator on the floor the main desk directed him to. He made a beeline for the nurse's station nearby. A petite, plump woman manned the desk.

"Can you tell me where Sharon Locker is?" he asked.

"She's in Room 328, just down the hall. Hang a left and

it's four doors down," the nurse said.

"Thank you."

Matt rushed down the hall, keeping himself from breaking out into a run. A message came over the hospital PA system for a Doctor Artovsky to pick up Line 2. Matt came to the door and stood there a moment. He wasn't sure he was ready to go in and see her like that. A small voice from the past whispered in his head.

"Momma, you don't need to worry anymore. I'll stand up for you. When I'm older, then I'll put you some place safe and I'll take care of you. I love you, Momma," a much younger, more innocent Matt said.

Matt went in the room. All sorts of tubes and wires fed into and attached to Momma. The soft beeping of the machine tracking her heartbeat seemed to fill the room. Momma looked smaller than normal, dwarfed by the apparatus around her. Matt pulled a chair next to her.

"Hey, Momma, I came as soon as I could. I'm so sorry I wasn't there to help you. I hope you weren't scared. I'm sorry I never made good on that promise to you."

Tears started welling up in his eyes again.

"Why would a loving God allow this to happen to you? Were you not faithful enough to Him? Why would He save him, just to take you away? Please don't go, Momma ..."

He couldn't stop the tears from falling.

"You know what really kills me? I meant to come see you a few days ago. I went and talked with that shrink you recommended. Dave said it would be good for me, too. Help me with some of my issues. I always thought that was what the gloves and a bag were for. Turns out, the shrink said that was part of the problem. Remember my buddy Jimmy?

"Jimmy and I were pretty good buds. We'd hang out, get in trouble together, all sorts of trouble. I was able to keep most of it from you, or so I thought, but you always knew, didn't you, Momma? What you don't know is why we stopped being friends. That day ..."

Matt went back to that day mentally. He and Jimmy were just heading back to Matt's house, after exploring the old Johnson place.

"Man, that old place is sure creepy. I can see why no one has lived in it in forever. Who'd want to live in a place where an old man killed his whole family?" Matt said.

"I think that might just be an old tale. Still, I was waiting for something to scare the shit outta us at any moment. Hey, are you going to the movies with us tomorrow night? Some of the other guys at school are all getting together to see that new action flick," Jimmy said.

"Naw, I don't have the money to go. Besides, I've got homework to get done or Ms. Eggels will have my head."

"Aw, come on, man! You can do homework on Saturday. If you need money, just lift some from your old man. He's so wasted most of the time, he'll never notice."

Matt's face hardened, looking like a miniature version of Darryl just then. His fist curled unconsciously.

"What did you say about my father?" Matt asked.

"I said lift the money from him, since he's always wasted. He won't miss it. What's wrong with you?" Jimmy asked.

"You take that shit back right now."

"Whoa, man. What? About your old man? It's the truth, though. Your old man is always drunkier than a fish in the Atlantic."

Matt advanced towards Jimmy, now both hands curled into fists.

"I don't care. You take that shit back."

Jimmy backed up from his bike, but stood his ground.

"No, man. I'm not doing it. It's the truth."

Matt flew at Jimmy. Matt's rage surprised Jimmy, and by the time the dust settled, Jimmy had a fat lip and already swelling eye. Matt looked at him and walked away.

"After that fight, we never spoke again. Even though he was right, it hurt so much to hear someone else say it about him. He's still my father, as much as I hate what he did to us. After that, I withdrew from a lot of the guys at school, and after Jimmy told them about the fight, they avoided me.

"Looking at it now, I can see now I failed in my promise to you. I swore that I wouldn't let a bottle control my life. But I am. I turn to violence because of this bottle of anger living inside that I refuse to let go of."

Matt sighed. He searched Momma's face for any gesture of understanding, of any sign she was waking up.

"Are you disappointed in me, Momma? I know you pray for me at every fight. I see the worry in your eyes before each one, the relief afterwards. Are you disappointed in the way I've turned out? You've never said anything, but I've always wondered."

There was a knock on the door, and Dave peeked in.

"Hey, Dave. Come on in."

Dave entered and sat in a seat by the window. The dark outside the window just was.

"Yer father was jus' 'ere. I told 'im that now wasn't prolly a good time ta see ya. 'E really wan's ta talk ta ya."

"I know, Dave. I just don't know how to face him without being angry. I feel like he took so much away from Momma and me. I can't forgive him for what he did."

"Ya can't say that, kid. Yer father's doing da best 'e can ta make amends. Try ta see things from 'is side."

"Hah. That's the problem. I was just telling Momma about the session I had with the shrink. How I realized I'm not that much different than my father."

"But yer diff'rent then yer da. Yer doing something with yer life. W'at 'e do?"

"Sure, that's what the shrink said. She said I was doing a good job sublimating the anger, using it to build a career. But the fact of the matter is that my life is still built around violence. Maybe I should forgive him. I guess I turned out just like him in a way."

"Don't be too 'ard on yerself, Matt."

Matt sat up suddenly as if something just occurred to him.

"W'at is it?" Dave asked.

"I just remembered something I had forgotten. It was one of the few times my father wasn't drunk. He had gotten some tickets from a friend for a football game ..."

It was a beautiful autumn day, that balance between brisk and warm, perfect for football. Matt got out of the car and started running into the yard, carrying a football.

"He jukes past the defenders, and past the goal line. Touchdown!"

Matt did a little victory dance, causing his father to laugh as he got out of the car himself.

"Yeah, Matt. That's how it's done. I take it you enjoyed the game?"

"Enjoyed it? Yeah. I mean, you came and got me early from school. We went to a football game, had hot dogs, nacho cheese, giant chocolate chip cookies. It was awesome."

Matt and Darryl began throwing the football back and forth in the yard. A group of kids passed on the street.

"I'm glad you had fun, son. I know things have been rough lately, and I'm sorry for that. I just want you to know that no matter what, I love you. Someday, when you're older, you'll understand."

"Sure, Dad. It's okay. I love you too."

Matt caught and held the ball.

"I just wish we had more days like this, Dad. Thank you."

Matt rushed over and hugged his dad.

"I know, son. Me too. Me too," his father said.

Matt quieted from the memory for a moment. The beeping filled the pregnant silence with presence, urgency. It was a little faster than before, though neither man noticed it.

"How hard can it be to say it? I forgive you, Dad," Matt said.

The beeping got faster, more insistent. Sharon sat up in the bed.

"Mattie?" she asked.

Matt rushed to her side.

"I'm here, Momma."

They hugged. As they did, Darryl peeked in the window of the door. Matt couldn't see him, but Sharon did. She could see the worry lines in his face. Matt barely heard her whisper.

"Thank you, God," she said.

Note on "Hitting the Bottle"

This story has had quite the evolution. After first learning about short shorts, or flash fiction, I tried it out. This taught me about the power of word choice and breaking the rules of grammar. I ended up producing a decent little story of 490 words.

Then I took a Theater Appreciation class. In the first week, my professor mentioned he judged a playwriting contest on campus, and since we were technically students, we could also submit an entry. I was intrigued, because I never thought to attempt a play script before. After class, I asked him for more information. It needed to be a one-act play of about 20 minutes. The deadline was the next week, but I figured I would give it a shot.

I adapted my short piece, then titled "The Fight," into about six pages of script. Through this experience, I learned more about dialogue and using it to move a story along. The next week, I turned in my few pages, apologizing for the shortness, and he said it was all right. He hadn't actually anticipated me submitting anyway. Fair enough.

After a few weeks, I learned my little script won. He said it had more going for it story-wise than the two other submissions did. Then I learned it had a $100 prize attached. I was just happy I won, but now I got paid! It was an awesome feeling.

The professor encouraged me to finish the play to the full 20-minute length and submit it the next year. I put it aside and out of mind for several months. Sometime during the summer break, it crossed my mind and I pulled it back out. Next thing I knew, two weeks had breezed by as I rewrote and expanded the original play. Finally finished, I asked a few people to read it. I wasn't ready for the reaction. It made a grown man cry. You ever have one of those moments when you suddenly have no idea what to do with yourself? It was like that. I didn't anticipate it actually resonating with people.

I submitted it to the professor through the mail (he wasn't teaching any classes at the facility that semester) and waited. I didn't hear a word back until February 2017, when I received a letter telling me I won again. Not only did it win, but it was first place on every judge's list out of eight submissions.

The school put on the play and I eventually was able to watch a recording of it. It was so well acted. I teared up watching it. I wrote it! I'm not supposed to cry, I knew what was coming.

I had considered just putting the script into this book, but then I read Harry Potter and the Cursed Child. This convinced me never to do this. While some people may enjoy reading scripts, I wish someone would have taken the time to novelize the story. This caused me to revert the script back into a story. It allowed me to tell the story a little more and to change some of the nuances of the story.

A lot of this story came out of my own frustrations with God and my troubled childhood. It wasn't the same, but I tried to convey a lot of the same emotions. I really just wanted to tell a realistic story, free of the horror and fantasy I usually write.

As a bonus, I've also included the original story. I hope you enjoy comparing the two.

The Fight

Red. The color fills the fighter's vision. Time slows. *Guy's fist's an anvil.* Too late to dodge or block. Pain impacts his face. He falls down

(blink)

and looks back up at his old man. His old man has a bottle of liquor in one hand and blood on the other. The kid feels his nose. It stings, his hand wet with blood.

"Stop it!" his mother screams.

"Shaddup!" his old man slurs. "You want some too?"

His old man steps over and slaps his mother. The sound echoes in the small living room. Something snaps inside the kid. A fire ignites. He moves to get up.

(blink)

"Two … Three!" counts the ref.

The fighter gets up. He can hear jeers in the crowd. He's the underdog, but doesn't care. He puts his gloves back up. Another minute.

"You good?" the ref asks.

The fighter nods. The ref motions for them to continue. The guy comes in fast. *This guy has too much energy.* The guy closes and throws several jabs. The fighter blocks or dodges, all but one. He thinks he sees an opening. He winds back. The uppercut surprises him mid-swing.

(blink)

knocking the kid to the floor again.

"What the fuck you think you're doing, piss ant?" his old man asks.

The kid looks at his mother. She cries quietly. A handprint is clear on her face. The kid stands up. The fire still blazes, reaching his eyes.

"Don't touch her again, asshole," he says.

His mother gasps and his old man's eyes widen.

"What did you say to me, piss ant?"

His old man's voice is quiet, dangerous. Fear rises like bile in his soul. He swallows it and stares his old man in the eye.

"I said, don't fucking touch her again, asshole."

The kid barely sees the fist coming towards him,

(blink)

but the fighter blocks the punch. He can see the guy thinks he's winning. *Hold on.* DING! Relief floods through the fighter. He makes his way to the corner. His trainer gives him tips, but the fighter barely hears him. He glances at his mother in the audience and

(blink)

between the punches, the kid sees the horror and helplessness on his mothers' face.

(blink)

The fighter faces his trainer. A fire re-ignites in his belly.

"He's cocky. Use it against him," his trainer says.

The fighter nods, standing up. The bell rings again. The fighter's world shrinks to just the guy. The guy never notices the change in the fighter's eyes, and lunges, sure it's the end. It is, but not for the fighter. The fighter sees an opening this time and side-steps. His counter flattens the guy. The ref counts to ten. The crowd cheers. His mother rushes to the ring,

(blink)

and while she holds the kid, he speaks.

"I love you, Mom."

(blink)

The fighter looks at the chaos around him. He looks up at the lights.

Thanks for the fight, Dad.

Fractured Minds and Lost Souls

POETRY

INTRODUCTION

Not a Poet

I'm not supposed to be a poet. It's my baby sister's thing. She already had some poems published in some random anthologies, though I don't know if she ever was paid for it, but she is able to put raw emotion on the page. You can't help but feel it.

I started doing poetry because I had to. I signed up for a Creative Writing course as part of my class load for my bachelor's. The first unit of it was poetry. I knew next to nothing about poetry. After some issues with getting the textbook, I decided to just grab a bunch of poetry books and read through them to start my education. I was exposed to Robert Frost, W.B. Yeats, Carl Sandburg, and so many others. I studied their poems, tried to figure out what made these poems great.

For some of them, I still have no idea. I found another book which broke down and explained the various forms, such as sestina, pantoum and villanelle (all of which have a sample in this collection, namely "The Sands Stay Though," "A Walk Among the Tombstones" and "A Moment for the Prisoner," respectively.)

After this, I started writing the poems I needed to for the class, but soon found I couldn't stop writing them. It seemed every other day gave some new inspiration to put to words. I wrote nearly all of the poems contained here in eight months. That number seems staggering to me.

I guess it's because I still don't consider myself a poet. I love to play with words, and writing a poem to a form is kind of like a borderless crossword puzzle. You have to find words that fit the idiom you're portraying and the rhyme scheme you're following. Then you have to ensure it evokes the same emotions you're trying to convey. Maybe the crossword analogy is bad, because this is sounding more like word alchemy. Yeah, that's it. In writing a poem, you can turn some crap words into gold. I hope you enjoy the poems.

Poetry

EVOLUTIONS and LIFE CHANGES

What is more enigmatic than a sunflower which opens at the break of day?
  Perchance more monolithic than a rampaging dragon that fills the
    Sky with fire and rage?
      What is marked by a dirge though its tempo indicates
        The occasion?
          I only know of two things so closely related:
          Marriage and death.

A HAPPIEST MOMENT

Solitarily entrenched, in need of a soul,
Nothing beholden to this wandering eye.
Chained long since the wintry sol
When rainbow colors danced the sky.

The collar around this neck, it wraps
Fear. Struggling for breath again.
Memory, naught but a remittent lapse,
Laughter from the immortal ken.

Attention crowds, captured in a gasp.
Beauty in full glory's dress.
Together with her father clasp,
Eyes killing the past loneliness.

Our souls touch with secret smiles,
Ready for the path, all the hard miles.

WORLD COVERED in SNOW

Cold, the house, the earth still under snow,
I pull on a sweater just to stay warm.
The fireplace is dim, filled with ash, unlit.

A cord of ash calls, all unchopped and neat.
I put on boots, coat, gloves and hat. Outward!

Boots crunch the snow, the frost nibbles at my cheeks.
In the darkening gloaming, the wind quiets.
Align the wood on block, arms take aim,

I take a moment, a second's pause, to
Ready my strength. Out of the blue, snowball!

Now I hear the laughter, a musical
Sound, neighborhood children hidden in forts.
Smiling at kids, I drive the axe through wood.

The kids return to their snow day war, as
I split wood for my nightly fire. Sweet warmth!

The whole of the wood fills quite an armload.
Reviewing the cosmos, the twilight dark.
My book calls inside, my work now is done.

The fireplace is lit, my book is nearby,
Two fingers of scotch, and my night is well!

The wood burns to ash, my boots are drying.
I take a sip, and feel the warmth fill me.
The kids have gone back to their homes, quiet now.
With book in my lap, here I sit 'til spring.

OF SNOW AND DREAMS

In the white, quiet stillness of the day,
A man found a piece of himself in the gray
   Of a mighty oak.
It spoke of hope and love and artistry,
There beneath that behemoth of a tree.

Its branches void of life and home,
He pulled out a brier pipe, used his fingers as a comb
   And started to smoke.
His fingers ran along the bark, breath and smoke streaming,
And found himself only dreaming.

This place was naught by sleep,
Paid to rest his darkness deep,
   Amidst evening's cloak.
As he continued down that country aisle,
The man began to regain his smile.

In passing the serious evergreens,
He thought of what that tree really means,
   Of the life it spoke.
He walked along, feeling old,
But saw his life's happiness unfold.

In the battered board nailed up high,
Embers ignited memories in his eye,
   As he drew upon the toke
And thought of building that ramshackle
Treehouse and all the games of tackle.

In the carved initials upon the trunk,
He thought of being in love and drunk,
   Evoking ghosts of Roanoke.
Life and love blossomed as the oak in spring.
In a room, her laughter would ring.

In the tattered rope from the bough,
He saw his daughter's smile, even now.
    This is where the dam broke
Because she had exchanged rings,
Taking to her new life on loving wings.

Still, boyhood had long ago cease,
And his love was in the ground at ease.
    Laughing at some private joke,
Despite his pain of loss steeped,
He laughed for all the happiness reaped.

BROTHER'S DUEL

A man's done wrong.
No law 'fore long.
Justice dealt strong
From the barrel of a gun.

They say violence
Ain't got much sense.
Good recompense
From the barrel of a gun.

Blind movement fast,
Moment don't last.
Each shot a blast
From the barrel of a gun.

We both shot true.
He gray, I blue.
Each got our due
From the barrel of a gun.

MAD REGENT'S HYMN

Bits of string, all unraveling,
It's separating at the seams.
Frayed purple clothing,
Nothing's no longer what it seems.

Times been a holy bastard too.
Moths and decay nip at the ends,
Hungry mouths all slaver and chew.
Courtiers never made good friends.

Clutching an old piece of metal,
Resting on my liar's chair.
Churches toll a sorrowful knell.
Red death banishes all who care.

But I have been a fiend as well,
Inscribing memento mori.
Bloody sword blade broken to hell,
Feeling, never saying, I'm sorry.

Laughing, the bards still sing my song.
Calamity, I could still bring.
I will continue to live long.
After all, I'm still King.

DEATH OF A GENTLEMAN BANDIT

I've had my last whiskey, and broken my bread.
Images of the noose still swim in my head,
But I sit waiting behind lock and key.

Sheriff says it's time, need to wear the ol' necktie.
This terrible end is mea culpa, by and by,
'Fore the day's end, I'll feel Death's rime.

The shackles twist and clang, a prelude to Hell.
I can hear the toil of a solitary bell.
Seems the whole town's come to watch me hang.

Still, the bell rings, and I march to the gallow,
Now, life doesn't seem all that shallow.
In the tree, a lone cardinal sings.

The noose 'round my head, my neck's against the rope,
Here, I'll hang 'til I'm dead,
But the lone cardinal gives me hope.

The sun warms my dead back; gone all the things I knew.
Despite all the good character I lack,
I look forward to beginning anew.

FOR THE DAMAGED

Black and white flags hang
Over silent greystones,
Alongside roaring steel horses,
From the porches of old men.
A stark reminder of four words:
We will never forget.

But what of those who appeared
To return whole, but in truth, in part?
Those minds left at the battle,
Still staring at the faces of dead friends,
They jump at the smallest sounds.
Do we forget these?

These fellows sit in life unfeeling,
Overwhelmed by unwanted memory.
They became alone and uncaring,
Yet able to rage into the dark night.
Bits of mind all unraveled,
Are they not damaged?

How about those who sit
Amidst brick and cage for crimes
Committed while their mind was AWOL?
Forever condemned for these times,
Decades of their life flow by.
Do we forget these?

These fellows become ghosts
Lost to world, but warehoused.
Trapped by their moments,
Moments of greatest regret,
Weakness shown but never owned.
Are they not missing?

Can we remember these men?
Can we bring them to Light
Of Joy and Love and Memory?
Remember the damaged
Remember the missing.
We will never forget.

A MOMENT for the PRISONER

Empty is the hall, not a person seen.
Echoing past bars and bricks, I hear doors slam.
Stillness for a prisoner, a rare scene.

Presently, the only human being,
Yet I am watched through a dozen minicam.
Empty is the hall, not a person seen.

Gone for the moment, all the guards in green.
Caged here for dishonoring Uncle Sam,
Stillness for a prisoner, a rare scene.

Cast out by country, fed to a machine,
Abandoned by all, no one gives a damn.
Empty is the hall, not a person seen.

Environment and rules, all to demean,
To shame the guilty criminal I am.
Stillness for a prisoner, a rare scene.

I know my value, despite what it may seem.
There's backbone and pride here, I am no lamb.
Empty is the hall, not a person seen.
Stillness for a prisoner, a rare scene.

BELONGINGS OF A PRISONER

Alone
This bed is a slab of stone.
Too many years since I've been home,
I long for the days when I can roam.

Sad
Left as a monstrous nomad,
I miss being a human being,
Though the world isn't seeing.

Rage
I sit here and only age.
Time travels forward, never back.
The anger drives the attack.

Guilt
For this cage I've kept built.
I have only myself and more to blame,
Nothing will ever be the same.

Alone, Sad, Rage, and Guilt:
Things a prisoner feels at full tilt.
Beneath it all, a small bit exists
Against the system, a prisoner resists.

Hope!
This alone is how prisoners cope.
With this, I can make it to utter end,
I can make our very spirits unbend.

DANGEROUS DIGRESSION

A threat of violence, a harshly spoken word
And the urge for digression returns with verve.
That dormant savage animal within
Stirs and growls in its mental captivity.

When this being in me awakes
I hurt those closest to me.
It slashes and snaps
And my life becomes combat.
I don't want to be scared.
I shouldn't be this way.

MOVEMENT IS EVERYWHERE

Sitting inside on a
Plastic blue lawn chair,
I face the outside
World, just watching.

Movement is everywhere.
Trees sway in the breezes,
Waving to each other as neighbors.
Emerald blades clash,
Always fighting for space.
Wildflowers bloom alone,
Crying out for attention.

Sleek black hornets buzz by,
Looking for last year's nest.
Butterflies float by,
Nature's aimless wanderers.
Beetles lumber through the grass,
A giant among their own world.

A distant hawk circles,
Surveying all from its tower.
Swallows chase around,
Playing grand games of tag.
Two ravens waddle,
Like businessmen in the park.
A redbird lands, throat open,
Pouring out its silence.

I watch life through five inch
Wide windows, cut off from
The movement and sound.
But I'm there in my heart.

A WALK AMONG the TOMBSTONES

Seeking relief from life, I went for a stroll.
My steps resonated, heavy with my dark plight
Past the quiet houses and buzzing lamps, I roll.
I look for a place to go deep in the midnight.

My steps resonated, heavy with my dark plight,
The lamplights' faded radiance guides my way.
I look for a place to go deep in the midnight,
Some place where the full dark holds perfect sway.

The lamplights' faded radiance guides my way.
My feet follow a path unseen to a dark graveyard,
Some place where the full dark holds perfect sway.
The place which holds, of me, that little shard.

My feet follow a path unseen to a dark graveyard.
It seems here that I find a thing sought, ethereal.
The place which holds, of me, that little shard,
A thing lost to the dark, but to me, fully real.

It seems here that I find a thing sought, ethereal;
A place of repose, here I am a burgess.
A thing lost to the dark, but to me, fully real.
Of quite solitude, I long for its address.

A place of repose, here I am a burgess,
But I seek not a path of eternal rest.
Of quite solitude, I long for its address.
Wisdom, I lay my head upon your breast.

But I seek not a path of eternal rest;
Here, I breathe the quiet amidst turbulence.
Wisdom, I lay my head upon your breast.
Please keep me in your sweet confidence.

Here I breathe the quiet amidst turbulence,
Upon storm-tossed seas, I rock and roll.
Please keep me in your sweet confidence,
Seeking relief from life, I went for a stroll.

THE SANDS STAY THOUGH (Sestina)

Lost, I am adrift in sand
And sheltered from midday sun, sit numb.
The computer conspires to bring me low,
My far-off love cries for what she typed.
Fissures in the façade; light flies from me;
Detached from affection, she wants divorce.

Stunned, I sit and think, "divorce?"
I rise and go stumbling into the sand
Looking for sweet Kat, a good friend to me.
"Dear Kat, I fear that I have become numb
And can't understand what my wife has typed.
Please, come read this before I sink too low."

A great friend, she can't bear to see me low
And so she reads that message of divorce.
She read those words, words most awfully typed,
While outside the vile wind tears, filled with sand.
She nods, tears welling. I fall, full numb.
Has love forever forsaken me?

Is fault wholly mine? My own blame seeks me.
I had no clue I could fall so damn low.
Days it takes to eliminate the numb.
O, how I hate that dreadful word, divorce.
Still, I do my job in Iraqi sand,
But at night, I fight for our love, I typed.

After the many missives written and typed,
I persuade her, other half of me
To wait 'til I return from land of sand.
Now I felt hope, no longer brought so low.
We speak of dreams again, not of divorce.
Now my ear was the only organ numb.

Finally, my feet have fallen asleep, numb.
"I'll be there for you waiting," she last typed.
Long gone were the messages of divorce.
In the gym, her eyes look right through to me.
Never again, I thought, would I be low.
Forward I move, leaving behind the sand.

But the sand is never gone, she falls back numb.
Though divorce is never typed, still I fail.
How could I know she would still bring me low?

THRICE-PARTED SORROW

I'll tell my tale 'fore I'm laid in a park,
Relate all my lost loves: my Fire, Light, and Dark.

Dark was my first real love,
Dark in her mood and gloom.
Dark, her family history.
Dark, the flesh inside her scars.

I was drawn, pulled to her darkness,
A moon to the dark planet orbiting.
Her darkness was soft, comfortable,
Pain and pleasure, both in equal measure.

Her pain made me protective, all love given,
I wanted to take her away from it.
I chose a path for her happiness,
But she misunderstood, fled, lost her way.

Time fades in sorrow's passage, but came a night,
Armed with a smile and a jest, I found my Light.

Light was my wedded love.
Light's presence filled a room.
Light needed a story.
Light's flaws were countless as stars.

I was blinded by her kindness,
A love of family and caring.
Her light was warm and beautiful.
Prayers and promises, made for the future.

Military career made us riven,
And wrote our marriage's obit.
My place in bed taken by a rat,
The love descended into a fray.

In my pain, I set my life on a pyre,
But my choices led to alluring Fire.

Fire was my secret love.
Fire's temper let her fume.
Fire never said sorry.
Fire's love was truly a farce.

She entranced me with raging fire,
Two souls in a passionate fling.
Her passion made me valuable,
Positions and prospects, fully explored.

But my crimes could not be forgiven,
Our flame was a brief respite.
All turned to ash and fell flat.
Now she disappeared, mysterious little fey.

Private, vital sorrows: Dark, Light, and Fire.
These are long gone. What love will next inspire?

BUBBLES

Soap, water, air
A thing created
Ephemeral, wondrous
Like the smile upon your face.

Dirt, water, sun
A time frozen
Eternal, blissful
Each little moment with you.

Dirt, leaves, rakes
A space built
Joyous, fleeting
Your laughter ringing in the trees.

Each moment a bubble
The time I spent with you
But moments only last
Like a child-caught sud.

REQUIEM AT THE OCEAN

Sitting by the ocean,
   Cool feet buried in sand.
Emotions are too heavy,
   No strength to stand.
Mind teleports to time,
   I gripped your little hand.
Listen to the waves, little
   Kay, surrah surrah.

Smiling back to present,
   Left with just the hurt.
Feeling our life at end,
   All laid under the dirt.
Stand, birds scattering,
   Wings fluttering, squawks blurt.
I'm stranded on shore alone,
   Que sera, sera.

LIKE IT WAS YESTERDAY

I was so nervous that day. I stood there, willing my stomach
to settle down, carrying two old pieces of precious metal
in my pocket. Your family was all around the room, just a few
short days from Christmas. I was due to get on a bus to the airport
to fly to Germany. You came running into the room, so happy
to see me. You tackle-hugged me. I told you we couldn't go
on that date I promised, but I said there was something else.
It involved the church next door. Unknown to you, it was
already decorated. Your family really got things together. It
involved these two rings I pulled from my pocket. These old
rings worn by my grandfather and grandmother. Your hands
covered your face. The rings fit. It involved your favorite cousin
in a flower girl outfit. She stepped into view. Everyone awwed.
I asked if you still wanted our wedding on the night we
planned. You said yes. Time and memory blurs to the point
I'm standing at the altar, your grandfather smiling at me from
behind his Bible. My new Army dress uniform uncomfortably
warm. You stepped into view on your stepfather's arm and
everything else faded. I couldn't keep the smile off my face.
Your beauty stole my ability to think. Then I looked you
in the eyes. Those beautiful, cloudless day blue eyes.
I said I do.

The years have been the wind between the hawk's talons.
A separation between a gulf unspeakable. Despite
these changes, I still hear your smile. I still dream
your face. Always have, always will.

NIGHT ESCAPE

The cricket calls, pulling the boy from slumber.
He sits quietly, eyes dilating for darkness.
Through the stillness, he feels the pull.
Quietly dressing, he's determined to escape.

Grabbing supplies for the journey,
He gets ready for the long descent.
Knowing these steps, he avoids the giveaway creaks.
He jumps the last few steps, landing to impress a cat.

He makes his way to a window looking into the world.
The night is everything, his life is not.
The window opens, quieter than the cursed door.
Bare feet touch feather-cool grass, he almost free.

He moves through the yard, sure no eyes can see.
He stops for a moment, appreciating his old friend.
This perfect willow hides the lair, his fort.
He quickly climbs the bastion of safety.

Here, there is no yelling, no knockdown family fights.
In this place, he's traveling back to the Second World War.
Reading the words of a girl trapped in an attic,
He knows exactly how she feels.

While reading of his time-casted love, a nearby rumble hums.
He dog-ears the page, anticipating what's coming.
The rumble grows while the horn screams its presence.
The boy sits enraptured with the simple night train.

Never moving, sound cocooning him, he's trainsported
Off to where these humble rails go, any adventure, any road.
The train like time keeps moving and soon it's far off.
Leaving the boy, just out of trance, a little off the rails.

With the behemoth gone, the crickets call out.
The boy returns to his escape, the book hiding his light.
Here he stays until the dawn kills the night
And he slinks back to captivity. He'll be back, come rain or sorrow.

ONLY AT THE PRECIPICE

They say we change ourselves at the Cliffside,
Doing all we can to save our hide.
What about those of us who, due to brokenness,
Miss all the warnings because of our arrogance?
All these people can't stop in time
End up looking back up at the climb.
Those people require the fall,
Must find themselves, losing it all.

At the bottom of this cliff is the real
Place of change, the impact we feel.
It's the choices here that show the person.
Choose the dark or climb to the sun.
Some choose to sit and fall apart,
But these ones show they have no heart.
Others choose to call for a rope,
But with helping hands, never learn to cope.

There are others still, rare to find,
Who do choose to climb. These are my kind.
These don't always climb right away.
They need some time to find their way,
But when the hands grip and their feet dig in,
This is where the real changes begin.
Here upon this Cliffside rough,
Is where we find the meaning of tough.

Sadly, not all climbers can endure
Or find their determination pure.
Some slide back when their hand bleeds
And so find themselves among the weeds.
Then those who find themselves in a bind
Prove they have no presence of mind.
They cry how they tried and mope.
These are left with little hope.

But those who made it back to the top
Found there was nothing to make them stop.
I have yet to achieve this victory
As I am still writing my history.

I will continue to push through,
I will be one that elevated crew.
All the while it will be a wild ride,
But I will look back upon this Cliffside.

THE INJURED ENDURE to SURVIVE

All rape is a transaction of power.
Behold, the one who takes it, the abuser.
"Innocence taken!" crys out the victim.

Secrecy, the haven of the abuser.
Blame and shame fly confused from the victim.
Perverse pleasure provokes this vile power.

Vengeance, justice, hope, sought for victims.
Hate, outrage, punishment, more for abusers.
A flipped script directs all the power.

So empowered, a victim overcomes all abusers and becomes Survivor.

YOU'LL NEVER KNOW

Stuck between a shadow and a gun,
These old ghosts flit at the corners.
The darkness beckons the soul.
Petrified by the hardened fear,
Fear of being alone.

Alone? This devil whispers inside.
There'll be so many others,
Others much more deserving.
A sweet music of agony and empty repentance.
A symphony playing for Eternity.
You'll never know the meaning of alone.

Stuck between radiance and a rail,
This shame narrows the vision.
The light summons the spirit.
Sickened by noxious fear,
Fear of being rejected.

Rejected? The angel shouts without.
He opened his arms for this,
Bled raging rivers of the Blood.
Shining choirs would welcome and enfold you,
A chorus singing His praises.
You'll never know the meaning of rejected.

Stuck between emptiness and a rope,
All seems a few shades darker.
Nullity envelops this fading spark.
Gutted by the sharpened fear,
Fear of being nothing.

Nothing? A small voice asks.
In this, there is only the whole.
All ceases within the void.
Vibrations flow across space,
Striking nothing with silence.
You'll never know the meaning of nothing.

Between these three states,
There's choices for the everlasting.
After contemplation and rumination,
A choice for life has been made.
You'll never know the meaning of death.

DRACONIAN HOSTILITIES

Emberant scales with inferno eyes,
Draconic rage flies overhead.
A return to his first domain
To find it claimed by another.

Scales of void coal and radioactive eyes,
Caustified bitterness in winged form.
She greets him with a sickly smile,
Lies and hatred flow vitriolic.

Vocal rage resonates in bone,
"You take what was never yours,
    Deny me my rights?
I've had my failures, these brought true ruin.
To heal the pain I caused, I search to
    Fail no more."

Acidic dripping whispers slide in the air,
"Leave with what you brought,
    This is all now mine.
The pain you caused left wounds gaping,
I stayed to heal, and this place changed.
    I rule this domain now."

His ire scorches, singes ill will.
"Eons have passed and stars have burned,
    Why do wounds still fester?
An overworked sense of vengeance?
True, a victim was wrought here,
    But it was never you."

Her venom flows, sizzling lively fire.
"Your flame caused great destruction,
        That much is true.
I have shaped this lair from its womb,
I was here as this all sprung forth.
        You are no elder."

Talons flashing, scoring rotten flesh.
"You lie uncaring in this cesspool,
        Bringing the land to rot.
Corruption heals when the source no longer holds.
I've flown to high places, while you sit
        Sowing your rancoric seeds."

Teeth shine, tearing heated marrow.
"This you will never rule again, I will
        Fight with all I am.
Your faults are still inside you, hiding
From the world and yourself, but the fact remains:
        I know you."

The conversation goes on, and does for an age.
Fire and acid both burn, but never mixing.
Still there is a question to contemplate:
Who is the more monstrous of the two?

IMMORTAL

The dark cast away
All surrounded by light
The insides are empty
People all around

Love and hatred
Numb by loneliness
An opiate
Waiting to kill

The bell rings hollow
The pews are full
The voices are lifted
But have no tone

Love and hatred
Numb by loneliness
An opiate
Waiting to kill
Leave it alone

The faces have smiles
The tears have eyes
The middle, a long step
A long goodbye

Love and hatred
Numb by loneliness
An opiate
Waiting to kill
Leave it alone
At the cliff's edge

Sunlight warms without
Void blows within
Self own eclipsed
Winter's begin

Love and hatred
Numb by loneliness
An opiate
Waiting to kill
Leave it alone
At the cliff's edge
Not willing to die

I'LL BE IRISH WHEN I DIE

In the hills of Kentucky,
You know where I was born,
I lived out in the Boonies
Where all's a little worn.
I couldn't stand the crazies,
But they grow the perfect rye.
So I'm drinkin' all the whiskey
'Cause I'll be Irish when I die!

Spent some time in Chicago
Where I met a lovely lass.
With hair afire and knuckles scarred,
She had her share of sass.
She caught me sleepin' 'round the town,
I thought that I could lie.
Now, I'm drinkin' whiskey through a straw
'Cause I'll be Irish when I die!

My luck's been down, you know
Of course, I've had a shitty year.
So I'll go on down to the corner
Pub and grab a round of beer.
I won't cry, no not a drop,
As the days go quickly by.
I'll drain my pint and throw my fist
'Cause I'll be Irish when I die!

I wasn't born an Irishman,
But I'm drinkin' all the beer,
And when I see a bit o' green,
I feel just a bit o' cheer.
I may end up in Hell because
I drink, I cheat and I lie,
But mark my grave with a Celtic cross
'Cause I'll be Irish when I die!

PROPOSAL TO HER

Wisdom, you're compared to a fine jewel
To be treasured more than finest gold.
Without you, I could only be a lovestruck fool.
Together, we could laugh and grow old.

Wisdom, I chased others, you were jealous,
Yet you're difficult to grasp, gossamer lace.
Others may see you as cold and heartless
But they don't know the shape of your face.

Wisdom, let me now approach
And offer you a love-stained tear.
All my inward parts, let me search
And assuage all my inborn fear.

Wisdom, I've sought you all my life,
Though the times I've loved you, too few.
There can be none better to love and wife,
A lovely woman with whom I start anew.

SEEKING, SEARCHING, LEARNING

Sitting in silence, still water calm
Allow for learning of hidden depths.
Simple waves obscure sight without qualm.

Inflame the passion in myself now.
Seeker of honest truth within wakes
Crystal clear mindful flame behind brow.

Forget that fearfulness cannot take,
Terror leads moreso to fearful self.
Master the monster mind, freedom's sake.

THE VOID AND THE FLAME

In the void, there is a candle
Burning brightly in my mind.
I focus 'til all falls away,
and there is only fire.
It burns, it heals.
It destroys, it renews.
The flame is not final.
Within the flame I go deep,
Deeper still than the light would betray.
In the deep, the flame far and round,
A crystal spins too.
Black and purple, dark within light;
Shatter the crystal, the shards make numb.
The flame gutters out.
In the void, I begin again.

SAVAGE LOATHING

Fly swiftly deep into that blazing night
Sober minds should fade at the close of day
Rage, rage against the coming of the light

Singapore Slings make for a blurry sight
Overlook the watermark from the Bay
Fly swiftly deep into that blazing night

Against the vicious bastards on the Right
Fight always, ensure the Freaks have their say
Rage, rage against the coming of the light

Acid makes mundane a terrible fright
Get out of town, escaping from the fray
Fly swifly deep into that blazing night

Chase the American Dream into flight
Looking for love, avoiding the DA
Rage, rage against the coming of the light

About everything, it must all be write
Back to Woody Creek, for sanity to stay
Fly swiftly deep into that blazing night
Rage, rage against the coming of the light

A MEASURE OF A MAN

Mighty is he who reaches out to
Aid, while in his own struggles,
Readily receives others' help.
Sure of himself, and ever willing to
Hear what others have to say.
Always ready with quick wit or fist,
Leading the charge into a fray,
Leaving behind none who go with.

Direct and determined, he keeps a hand on the bow,
Righting the course of his life,
Adjusting others along the way. He
Keeps a weather eye on the horizon and is
Everything a pirate and man should be.

WILD FEY LOVER

You danced in wild fey circles with murder in your eyes
Rejoicing for the pools of blood you've left far behind.
Sadism lies masked within you, under beautiful guise,
Gorgeous darkness coiled in the lacuna of your mind.

For all the pain you've inflicted, I can't help but love.
A dog to its vomit, my mind circled 'round to you.
To you, my agony was sweet; to me, t'was foxglove.
Of your fits of loving kindness, I've seen far too few.

Unlucky in love, was this my overserved dessert?
Your cruelty, something I could no longer abhor?
I slumbered and indifference inflicted more hurt;
Despite the fight, I endured. I've absorbed so much more.

Your passion in season, but your glacial hand has bite,
My strength slumbers as a bear on a winter's day.
You wielded all demands, decreed me submit without fight,
But you'll never have all of me, lovely little fey.

MY OWN CATHEDRAL

Daffodils
The yellow-toothed gods of the prairie
Preside over their abandoned open-air hall
Waves ripple as tho' wind-tossed sea
The cold wind's a harbinger of the fall

The Elm
That wizened, old, ancient tree
Whiles the time past eternal
Never have I seen a tree so lonely
Yet stand up so frightfully tall

An Old Stone
The markings far too faded to see
A memento of the final funeral
Silent, it bears no obvious plea
Its mere presence reminds all

The Young Man
Sits so solidly within the old tree
Joining this company in the sacred hall
In truth, it's just little ol' me
Patiently waiting for the days of fall.

A CONTINUING JOURNEY

Floating through the lost aeons,
A speck of dust, vast universe.
Searching for elusive Higgs-Bosons,
Space cannot be bound in verse.

Bumbled, bobbled, wheedled about,
A cosmic tumbleweed gathering speed.
Random bearings have been sought out
There, now exists a nameless need.

Light, all awash in color and summer,
Aware, alone to the warmth and dark.
Beyond sight beats faceless drummer,
Feeling safe and sacred as an ark.

Time blinks, the enclosure presses in,
The light blinds unseeing eyes.
Self reestablished, I'm born ag'in.
Life anew in the family ties.

AN ENCOURAGEMENT

Reality is insanity,
Of this, there is no doubt
All of life is vanity,
Some just need a way out.

About these things, you cannot pout.
You need face yourself, be stronger,
Believe you'll win this next bout.
Remember, though, this isn't Frogger.

After all, good comes after danger,
But you only have the one life.
So settle in, unmake the Stranger,
These are all the facts of life.

A LINK TO THE PAST

Down in the basement
Lost among the boxes,
I find an old gray box of joy.
Smiling at the hours
I sat tethered to its face.

I open the lid to find
A surprise still inside.
A cache of gold with
A well-worn melody.
I bring this treasure to my lair.

Having adjusted the screen
For this old box of memory,
I give it the push
It needs for power.
My smile lights up.

I quickly find the cave
Where a strange old man
Hands me a sharp sword.
It's dangerous to go outside,
But I'll rescue the princess yet again.

MY COUNTRY, PLEASE LISTEN

America, we're in a bad spot.
We haven't been united since 9/11.
What's really going down?
Christians hiding in churches,
Cops killing in the streets.
The government is nowhere to be found.
How much do we have to pay
For our children to eat?
This life is not very sound.
Black lives matter and march,
While rednecks drown in meth.
The problem we have is not race,
It's really a matter of class.
With truckers earning just pennies,
The rich are trying to save face.
The Mexicans are being deported,
And the Arabs are all but banned,
What happened to our great melting pot?
Our division strikes deeper
And protests growing violent,
We're heading to war at a trot.
My country, please listen,
We need to correct our course
Or under the tide, we'll drown.

WRITTEN PARAPHERNALIA

Empty pens and bits of dead tree
Litter my fortified space.
Unborn stanzas and hieroglyphic notes
Mock my letter-worn face.

Radio's cycling through the stations,
Listening for the muse's whisper.
A darkness haunts the room
Like a not-so-friendly Casper.

Nothing meets the evaluation
With my word bank on E.
Phrases elude and escape,
Where's the word I want to see?

Things I feel and want to say
Seem to have already been said.
These ideas, my soul invests itself
To them, words of writers long dead.

Despite the passage of time,
The old clichés still ring true.
How long does it take
For wisdom again to be new?

Perhaps the world is too much,
I'm too full of mindfulness.
Within my chosen path of self,
I'm overtaken with madness.

Resigned to the search
Despite this infernal frustration,
I hunker down here waiting for
The lexocological solution.

DAUGHTER, HEAR YOUR FATHER NOW

I loved you before your first cry, before your first smile.
Daughter, hear your father now, I long to reconcile.
When I first held you, I couldn't speak a word.
Endless words in mind, I didn't think I'd be heard.
But so soon after you arrived, I had to leave.
I missed you every day; for a year, I grieved.
Coming back, my joy and smiles resumed.
With you, my life felt perfect and illumed.
When you took your first steps, I was overbursting with pride.
For each of your little victories, I stood there, moist-eyed.
But the time came again when I was taken to the land of sand.
I thought of you every few seconds as you grew in Rhineland.

Through the stress and the troubles, I came home a different dad.
Before a year was passed, I did something terribly bad.
My horrific actions preyed on my soul, made me want to run.
I hurt you, something which could not be undone.
You said, "If Dad said he was sorry, I'd be okay."
I wept and your love killed me, my darling Kay.
I added another chapter to our dark family history.
Daughter, hear your father now, I am so very sorry.

Fractured Minds and Lost Souls

NOTES ON POETRY

"Evolutions and Life Changes"

The sentiment in this poem is true. The song played for weddings and funerals is the same, just the tempo is different. Is this really so strange? We link marriage and death together quite strongly. We hold bachelor and bachelorette parties which "mourn" the death of our "single" lives. We vow to remain together in matrimony, "till death do us part." Maybe this says some uncomfortable things about the institution of marriage.

"A Happiest Moment"

I'm kind of a hopeless romantic. Being in love is a great feeling, but when you add commitment, there's a bit of terror as well. It takes experience for us to understand what love is and means. I only hope I have another chance at it in the future.

"World Covered in Snow"

I wrote this from a poet game I read about, called "Spring Running." Certain words connect each stanza, with all of these connecting words used in the last stanza, or envoi. The envoi also has to mention spring. I wanted to write something peaceful, because a lot of what I tend to write is pretty dark. I asked what a simple, peaceful day for myself would look like. Not to mention, winter is my favorite season. I love the cold and snow. I love the holidays where people are kind to one another. Many of my best and happiest memories come from the month of December.

"Of Snow and Dreams"

This is another one born with a half-sleep state. It turned into the first three stanzas. Then a friend asked what was in the tree that made the man smile. It turned into a reflection of life; despite the pain and loss we suffer, there's so much brightness and happiness we receive from the deal.

"Brother's Duel"

I was experimenting with purposefully writing in a historical persona when this was written. It was initially a couple of stanzas longer, but I removed them because they really weren't needed. One of the things I like the most about this poem is the sense of righteous anger and vengeancy played out through, though what the slight was, even I don't know.

"Mad Regent's Hymn"

This was one of those poems that came to me just as I was about to sleep. I love how the persona developed. I had it written in one sitting with very little revision afterwards. I love how tired and worn he sounds, with just a tinge of regret, but still having that noble pride.

"Death of a Gentleman Bandit"

This is about regret and hope. I wrote this while rereading *The Gunslinger* by Stephen King, hence the Western idiom. I say the persona here is a gentleman bandit, because he clearly has some Catholic learning, but has his uncouth side. I tried to have that come out through the way he speaks in each line.

"For the Damaged"

Sitting in a military prison with so many who have deployed and seen combat in the last two decades is a sobering thing. I feel we should be doing more to honestly treat these men, instead of just giving it all lip service. I also wanted to address the overseverity of the military justice system. Unless you've had any dealings with it, you have no idea how soulless it can be.

"A Moment for the Prisoner"

This one sprang up while I was walking from the mental health offices in my facility back to my housing unit. This requires walking down this long hallway. It usually has a ton of traffic, since it's the main thoroughfare for the facility.

At this particular time, it was just me in the hallway. It was pretty unusual. Luckily, I had my notebook on me at the time, and I started scribbling down notes as I was walking. At one point, guards came out of an office and walked past me, asking me what I was doing. I had to explain that I had suddenly gotten an idea for a poem and was writing it down. I recognize I probably looked a little crazy, writing and walking at the same time, but oh well. I've often questioned my amount of sanity.

"Belongings of a Prisoner"

Prisoners don't really own anything. We don't own the clothes on our backs anymore, the food in our stomach. At any time, for any reason, what little we have can be taken from us. The only things we can keep, and can never be taken from us, are our thoughts and feelings. I wanted to acknowledge this struggle for American prisoners everywhere. Come get me, thought police!

"Dangerous Digression"

When I was younger, I had a huge problem with anger. While I've learned to control it mostly, life constantly tests the limits, especially in prison. It seems the more you let frustration build up, the easier it becomes to revert to this animalistic mindset. It takes a constant effort to be something better.

"Movement is Everywhere"

When you're sitting in a prison cell, you can get the feeling that everything and everyone is moving, except you. I sat at my window one day, watching the little bit of nature I can see. I wanted to document it, record that feeling of seeing it and wanting to be out there too.

"A Walk Among the Tombstones"

This was one of my favorite things to do during my senior year of high school. On nights where I just needed to think for a while, I headed to the cemetery. I find it peaceful in a cemetery at night. I used to worry what this said about me, but then I sent a copy of the poem to my great-aunt. She explained that my grandmother and she used to take walks through the local cemeteries as well. This became a connection to my family past, as my grandmother sadly passed away when I was 13. She would have liked this poem.

"The Sands Stay Though"

During my second deployment, a fifteen-month tour in Iraq, this happened. Why is this story important? This is where a much larger narrative starts, a narrative about my descent into the darkness which led me to being incarcerated.

Some good did come from this particular trouble. As I struggled to save my marriage, I was unwittingly encouraging others to work on their marriages as well. After the unit arrived back home, a few couples approached me and thanked me for my example. I guess this is what people mean when they say, "God uses your pain for His glory." Small comfort for such a big pain.

"Thrice-Parted Sorrow"

The title is a reference to Shakespeare's line, "Parting is such sweet sorrow." I'm not sure I agree with that sentiment. Leaving a loved one for any reason hurts. This was written about the three women I feel I've truly and romantically loved in my life. I believe each real relationship leaves an impression on us and who we are. As men, we carry those women we've shared our lives with for the rest of our lives.

"Bubbles"

I formatted this to reinforce the image of bubbles floating away. It started out being just about spending a summer day blowing bubbles with my daughter in the yard and hearing her infectious laughter. As I wrote it, I realized there were so many of these moments we miss until they're gone. Sad, really.

"Requiem at the Ocean"

A friend once played Doris Day's "Que Sera, Sera" for me, and I thought it was a beautiful song. "Whatever will be, will be. The future is not ours to see." I wrote this, thinking about the weekend I spent in Ocean City, Maryland, alone.

"Like It Was Yesterday"

This prose poem I wrote to express what I truly felt for my ex-wife, despite all the pain and heartache we've been through. It's a beautiful memory I'll always cherish.

"Night Escape"

This was me. At one point in my life, my mother felt she had to ground me from books. Grounding me to my room wasn't helpful, because I would just sit and read. We didn't have the best family dynamic. I wanted to tell a personal story, but tell it from an outsider's point of view.

"Only at the Precipice"

In the remake of the movie *The Day the Earth Stood Still*, John Cleese has this wonderful line, "Only at the precipice, do we change." It referred to how we as humans really only change ourselves when we sense our lives are in danger. However, I realized this wasn't universally true.

"The Injured Endure to Survive"

Rape is a terrible, horrible subject. I wanted to write this as an encouragement to all of us who have survived any type of sexual abuse. I formatted it to simulate a swinging pendulum to show a balance upset. Such a terrible act can cause lives to be set wildly into motion. Eventually, it can balance out, but if you aren't careful, the balance can still be askew, making it easier to become unbalanced.

"You'll Never Know"

I've thought about suicide a lot. Still, I've found that it's always hope that keeps me going. Hope that tomorrow will be better. While there are setbacks, I've never been disappointed by this hope. When you're in a dark place, you might hear the siren call of suicide, to just end it and let the pain go away. It seems we hear these voices, all vying for our attention and souls. Perhaps, it might be better if we keep our soul instead?

"Draconian Hostilities"

At face value, this is a conversation between a red dragon and a black dragon over a domain. In reality, it's a metaphor representing two sides unable to forgive each other. That kind of environment is terribly caustic and leaves horrendous scars.

"Immortal"

This was written before I knew much about poetry. I was dealing with soul-crushing depression. I felt empty, cut off from everyone around me. I was tired of fighting all the time, but I recognized I wanted to keep living despite the pain and loneliness. I wrote the chorus so that each pair of lines made a separate thought, such as "Love and hatred/ Numb by loneliness" and "Numb by loneliness/An opiate." I tried to pack the emotion I was feeling within all of those pairings, and each time the chorus repeated, I added a line, further clarifying the emotions, until the final ending line, "At the cliff's edge/Not willing to die."

"I'll Be Irish When I Die"

I love the Irish. There's a toughness to them that never quits. I identify as Irish, even though I'll admit I'm not exactly sure as to my ancestry on this. My grandmother's maiden name was Campbell, which is an Irish name, so there's bound to be some. Still, I just wanted to try to write a pub song. Did I succeed? We'll see if I ever hear someone singing this in a pub.

"Proposal To Her"

In the Bible, Wisdom is personified as a woman. Wisdom is something I've sought my whole life. I read the book of Proverbs daily. When I was 12, I first read the story of Solomon asking God for wisdom, and for some reason, I wanted that too. I prayed for it. God's never just given me wisdom, but He has given me plenty of opportunity to learn it. My courtship with her will likely continue until I die.

"Seeking, Searching, Learning"

This is about meditation, learning to look inside yourself and be still. It's a hard skill to acquire, especially since every time I went to do it, my brain started spewing hateful self-talk. The trick is getting it to shut up. I limited the syllables in each line to nine, in a nod to the odd syllable counts haikus and koans usually have.

"The Void and the Flame"

This is another poem about meditation. It was influenced by Robert Jordan's *Wheel of Time* series. The main character, Rand, uses a technique to put himself in the right state of mind for his swordsmanship and spellcasting.

"Savage Loathing"

This is a parody of Dylan Thomas's "Do not go gentle into that good night," as well as an homage to Hunter S. Thompson. I had never read anything by HST until I was incarcerated, but now I read everything I can get my hands on.

According to an interview HST did with *The Paris Review*, he had a banner in his office, written in his own hand, twisting the last line of the Thomas poem, "Rage, rage against the coming of the light." I thought it was an interesting sentiment, and tried to write a poem that referenced much of his work. I can only hope he would have been proud of it.

"A Measure of a Man"

I wrote this for a friend for his birthday. He's a bit of an honest jerk, but he's reliable and loyal. In other words, a damn good friend. He's also completely in love with pirate lore, being descended from the great Sir Francis Drake himself. This is hilarious to me, considering he was an Army Infantryman.

"Wild Fey Lover"

Fairy folklore is fascinating. They're beautiful, yet cruel creatures, almost alien to the human mind. Like some women I knew. Still, I wanted to recreate the feelings of a bad relationship you can't seem to pull away from, but you guard a piece of yourself, fighting complete submission. It's a sentiment I've felt and heard others speak about, though I agree it's not the most rational thing. We humans are rarely rational.

"My Own Cathedral"

I like being alone at times. That's not to say I don't like people. They're fascinating, but sometimes they can be a bit much and I need time away. The start of this poem came from a friend as we were mocking slam poetry, except when he said this, we both realized it was actually kind of a cool line. I told him I was going to steal it, and built the poem from it. He was happy with the result, mostly because he's a curmudgeonly introvert.

"A Continuing Journey"

I've often given thought to what it would be like to be

reborn physically. One of my favorite movies, W*hat Dreams May Come*, touches on this (also note the previous hopeless romantic comment). Would we remember our former selves at all? Obviously, we forget who we were at some point. I can already hear my Christian friends saying, "That isn't biblical." No, it isn't, it's just a thought in an imaginative mind.

"An Encouragement"

I wrote this little bit just trying to be funny. If you've ever read the book Ecclesiastes in the Bible, you'd recognize the sentiment in the first stanza. Life can be pretty absurd.

"A Link to the Past"

Before I was incarcerated, I was attending school to become a game designer. I love video games, and they've nearly always been a part of my life. They're a rich, interactive storytelling platform. Alas, I'll never realize that dream, but I still think about games fondly, especially the old RPGs like *The Legend of Zelda*, *King's Field II* (PSI), and *The Elder Scrolls: Morrowind* (Xbox).

"My Country, Please Listen"

I'm a junkie for news, especially with the restricted access to it in prison. Even still, I'm starting to hate how much anger and division I see in our own country. We can't seem to agree on anything. "The times, they are a-changing," and all I can do is write about it.

"Written Paraphernalia"

I legitimately wrote this out of frustration while trying to write another poem. I wanted to convey that feeling of frustration writers often encounter when they're working, worried about whether they've gone insane of not. I know I often feel slightly off, but we can't all be insane, right?

"Daughter, Hear Your Father Now"

This is probably my most honest and raw poem of the bunch.

Acknowledgments

There are so many people I have to thank for the existence of this book.

First, I'd like to thank God, because that's my belief, and that's how it's done.

I'd like to thank my publisher/editor, Ann Miller, because she believed in me enough to say, "Let's do this."

Thank you to all the teachers who've encouraged me along the way: Dr. Michael Waller (for not going easy on me), Dr. Charles Leader (for believing even a prisoner can participate), Mrs. Angela Consani (get your doctorate already!), and Dr. Carol Guerrero-Murphy (I might not always like your feedback, but it has always been good).

Lastly, but surely not least, to many of the men within the USDB. Many of you guys suffered through as first readers and gave valuable feedback, not to mention wild encouragement: Marshall, George, Phlynxe, Jeremy, Josh, Jacob, Dan, Maurice, Jesse, Brad, Jason, and so many others, and to all those who are no longer at the USDB, but had a hand in this as well.